LOVE ORIGAMI

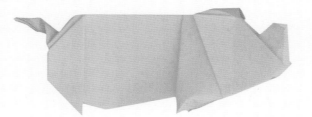

An Hachette UK Company
www.hachette.co.uk

First published in Great Britain in 2017
by Mitchell Beazley, a division
of Octopus Publishing Group Ltd
Carmelite House
50 Victoria Embankment
London EC4Y 0DZ
www.octopusbooks.co.uk

QUAR.SOGM

ISBN 978-1-78472-362-0

A CIP catalogue record for this book is
available from the British Library.

Conceived, designed and produced by
Quarto Publishing plc
6 Blundell Street
London N7 9BH

Editor: Kate Burkett
Design: Wide Open Studio
Art director: Caroline Guest
Creative director: Moira Clinch
Publisher: Samantha Warrington

Printed in China
10 9 8 7 6 5 4 3 2 1

LOVE ORIGAMI

20 Simple Paper Projects To Fold, Style & Share

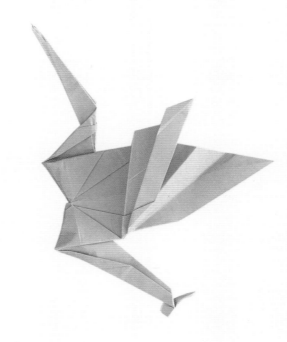

ROSS SYMONS

MITCHELL
BEAZLEY

CONTENTS

WELCOME TO MY WORLD

Hi there :) My name is Ross and I am an accidental origami artist. I say accidental because I never intended on becoming an artist at all, not until I started a project on Instagram in 2014. It was a year-long project whereby I folded and photographed a new origami shape every day of the year and posted it onto the social-media channel. I was fortunate enough to gain a large following and, as a result, I quit my job and became a full-time origami artist. This kicked off my career as an artist. I now design origami products, create hanging and wall installations for brands and companies around the world and make short origami stop-motion animations for social-media campaigns.

I love folding paper and creating animations. Paper listens to what you ask it to do, but only if you understand it. By using the right paper and knowing its limitations, you can create anything. I'm also really passionate about connecting with people all over the world. My greatest inspiration is seeing others use their creativity to grow and be happier, as I have done. I look forward to connecting with you through the projects in this book, which I have designed for you to create.

'Once you understand the fundamental elements of what you have to work with, a universe of possibility opens up. It forces you to look past what you think you know about something – in this case a piece of folded paper.'

For me, one of the most inspiring elements of origami is its limitation. You start with a sheet of paper and fold it. That's it. You might think that because of this limitation you are unable to be creative, but I find it's quite the opposite. Once you understand the fundamental elements of what you have to work with, a universe of possibility opens up. It forces you to look past what you think you know about something – in this case a piece of folded paper. Something else I love about origami is how the concept of folding and foldability has moved into many other industries, such as medicine, industrial design, space travel and interior design. To see this in practice is just fantastic. Why not take a day and note all of the things you interact with that fold? I'm sure you'll be amazed.

'Believe.'

EIGHT REASONS WHY I LOVE ORIGAMI

I love origami because, using just one piece of paper, I can create something that puts a smile on someone's face.

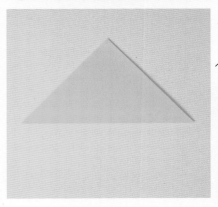

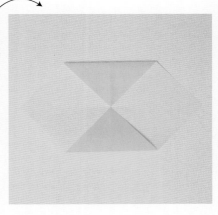

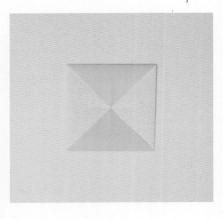

I love origami because it's so easy to pull out a sheet of paper and start folding – whether I'm in a queue, sitting having coffee or waiting for a friend.

I love origami because the only tools I need are my hands and a square piece of paper. So, when inspiration strikes, I can get going wherever I am.

I love origami because paper is very obedient. It listens to everything you ask it to do, but only if you understand its folds and limitations.

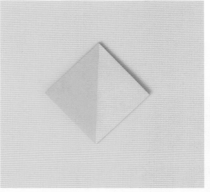

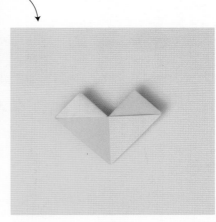

I love origami because it has taught me how to be patient and persistent. If you don't get it right straight away, you just have to grab more paper and start again.

I love origami because it was just a hobby and now it's my full-time job. Origami has made me realise that if you are willing to work hard, you can create a career out of anything.

I love origami because it takes time. You cannot skip ahead to step 10 if you haven't folded steps 1 to 9. Knowing the process and taking it step-by-step reminds me to slow things down and enjoy the ride.

I love origami because it's meditative. I use my mind and my hands to focus all my attention on one thing.

'Everything else disappears and I feel calm.'

GALLERY OF WORK

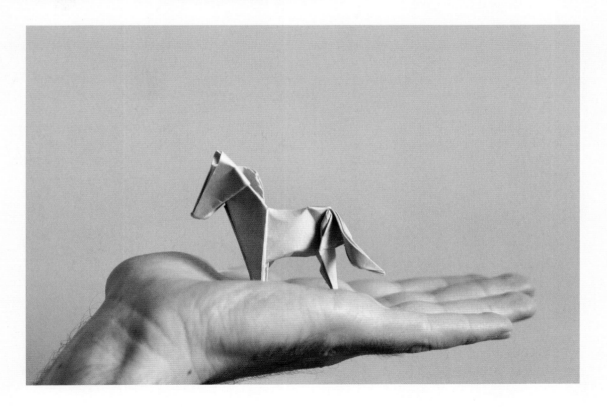

'Eat, sleep, fold, repeat.'

The pony (left) is one of my earliest designs. I took this photo as part of a colour series I did on Instagram called 'Colourgami'. The flying cranes photo (above) was the final shot of my 365-day Instagram project. It took me about half an hour to get the picture right since I had to make sure the light was perfect.

I folded these two zebras and pink unicorn (above) for a client and, when I saw them together, I had to take a quick snap. I wonder what the zebras said to make the unicorn so sad?

I folded these giraffes (left) for a wedding and decided to create a safari scene with all of them together. A group of giraffes is called a tower – did you know that?

A pink unicorn will always take the cake (see what I did there?)! This delicious cake was made by my lovely girlfriend, Nikki, and I added the unicorn topping (right).

'This is what I get up to on my days off. Unicorns, pink cakes and flying sprinkles!'

I folded unicorns (above) for a baby mobile I made for a friend and the idea of an epic unicorn journey came to me when I saw them all together.

I love using colour to bring out the features in a piece. The blue background works really well with the ivory zebra and giraffe (left).

A fleet of foxes (above). No, wait, it's actually called a leash of foxes.

The rhino (right) is the first of the big five game animals I've designed – I hope to create models of all five at some point.

'I enjoy creating origami that is simple, but captures the essence of the creature.'

'I carry paper with me at ALL times. You just never know when inspiration might strike.'

A lot of my photography work is quite minimal and clean. These little sparrows (left) are a great example of that.

This bull (below) is folded from elephant hide, which is usually used for book binding. It is my favourite paper to fold with.

Nothing to see here – just a rabbit hopping onto a spacebar (right). This was taken for an Instagram campaign I did for an electrons company.

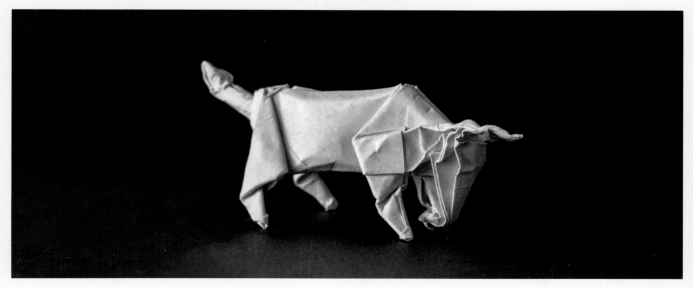

BASIC FOLDS AND BASES

Here are the basic techniques you will need to complete the designs in this book. You should practise these with scrap paper until you understand them fully. Try altering angles and distances to see how it affects the result. No matter how complex they are, all origami designs are made up from these simple sequences. The symbols (below) are used with the photographic steps.

PROJECT KEY:

The mountain fold
is shown by a blue dash-dot line.

The valley fold
is shown by a red dashed line.

Fold in this direction
is shown by a fine arrow.

Fold and unfold
is shown by a fine arrow
with two arrowheads.

x
indicates exactly where to fold to.

Flip model: **Rotate model:**

 FLIP

EQUIPMENT:

These are my go-to origami tools:

+ **Pencil** – Used to mark off a square on a non-square sheet of paper.

+ **Bone folder** – Instead of using my hands, I often use a bone folder to fold so the paper stays clean and has sharper folds.

+ **Tweezers** – Different types of tweezers are great for achieving different results. I use flat nose tweezers, for example, not only to flatten a crease, but also to hold the paper while I fold another section of the model.

+ **Ruler** – Not just for drawing straight lines – I sometimes use this tool as another method of creasing paper.

+ **Cutting knife** – Coupled with a ruler, this is great for cutting out square sheets of paper.

+ **Scissors** – Comes in useful when you want to curl the edges of the paper slightly.

+ **Bulldog clips** – When I use a wet folding technique, I use bulldog clips to hold the paper in place.

+ **Pen and felt tip marker** – Ideal for adding little extras to some of my designs, such as eyes or a nose.

MOUNTAIN

Fold the paper away from you so it folds underneath the line shown.

The result.

VALLEY

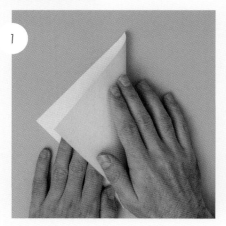

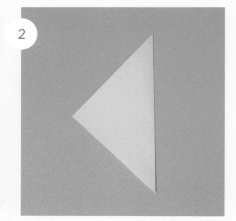

Fold the paper up towards you and down along the centre.

The result.

OUTSIDE REVERSE FOLD

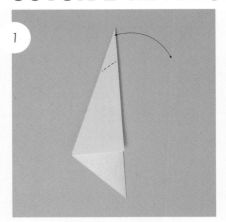

1

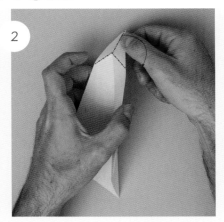

2

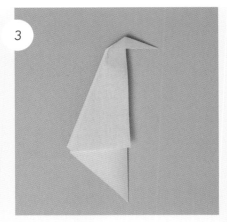

3

The point of this fold is to bring the tip down over the outside of the model. Start by creating a valley fold and unfold it along the line shown.

Fold the tip down. The previous valley fold becomes a mountain fold on both sides of the model.

The result.

INSIDE REVERSE FOLD

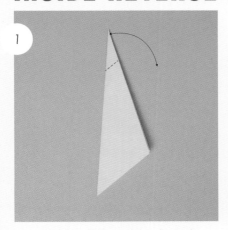

1

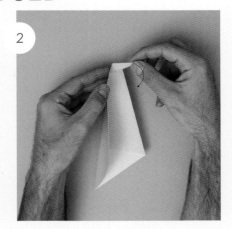

2

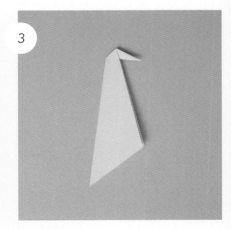

3

The point of this fold is to bring the tip down through the inside of the model. Start by creating a valley fold and unfold it along the line shown.

Fold the tip down. The previous valley fold will become a mountain fold.

The result.

WATER BOMB BASE

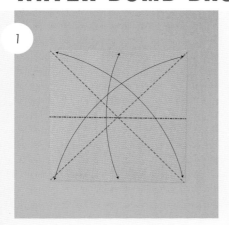

1

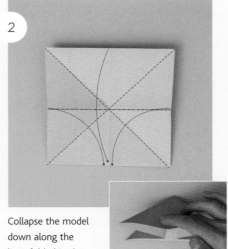

2

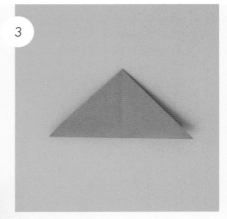

3

With white side up, valley fold and unfold from corner to corner on both sides, then mountain fold a line through the centre along the line shown.

Collapse the model down along the lines folded in the previous step.

The result.

KITE BASE

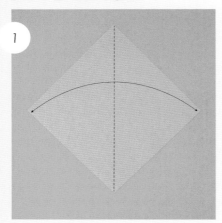

1

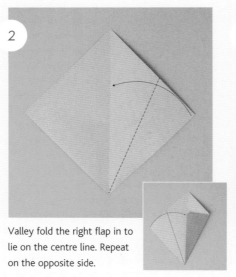

2

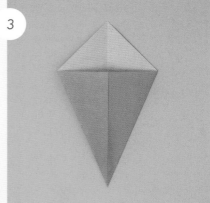

3

With white side up and on a diagonal, valley fold and unfold a line through the centre.

Valley fold the right flap in to lie on the centre line. Repeat on the opposite side.

The result.

BIRD BASE

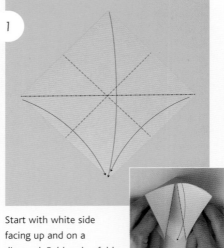

1 Start with white side facing up and on a diagonal. Fold and unfold along lines shown, open sheet up, then collapse model down to bottom point.

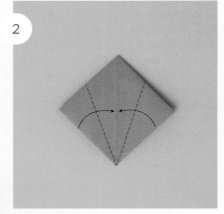

2 Fold the top flaps into the centre line.

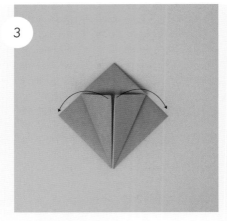

3 Unfold flaps back to step 2.

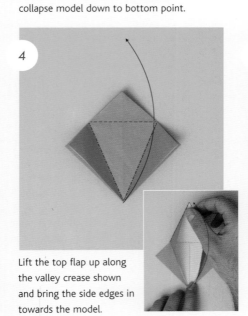

4 Lift the top flap up along the valley crease shown and bring the side edges in towards the model.

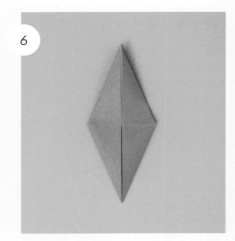

5 Repeat steps 2, 3 and 4 on the flap behind.

6 The result.

FISH BASE

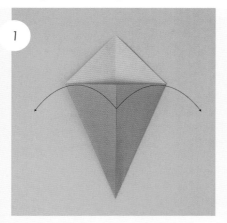

1

Start with a kite base and unfold flaps out.

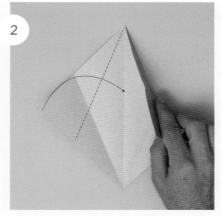

2

Valley fold left and right edges from top point to centre line along lines shown.

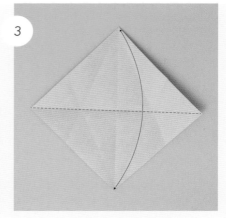

3

Valley fold and unfold bottom point to top.

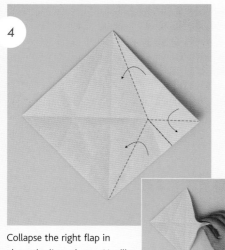

4

Collapse the right flap in along the lines shown. You'll notice that a new mountain fold will form as the flap closes.

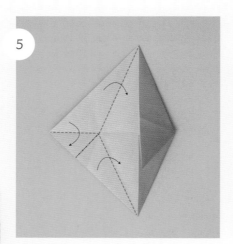

5

Repeat step 4 on opposite side.

6

The result.

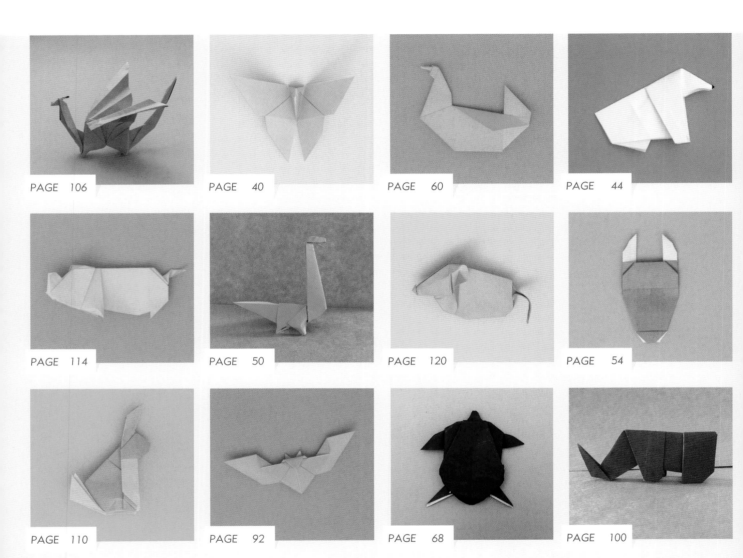

ROSS'S FAVOURITE FOLDS...

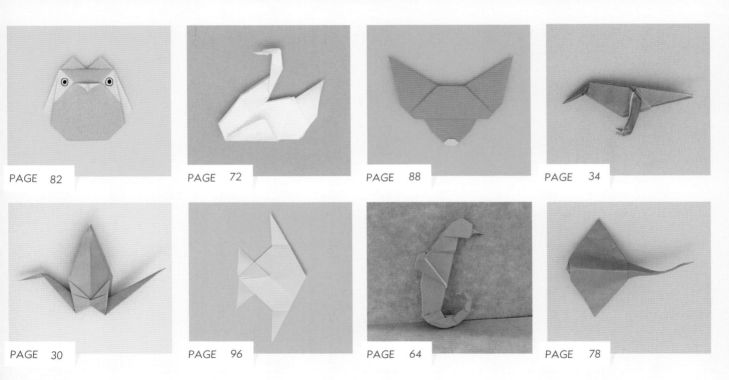

PAGE 82

PAGE 72

PAGE 88

PAGE 34

PAGE 30

PAGE 96

PAGE 64

PAGE 78

CRANE

The crane (or 'tsuru' in Japanese) is the symbol of origami.
This is usually the first design that gets mastered as it uses
many of the beginner origami folding techniques - valley,
mountain, reverse and petal fold. Thin paper is best for this
design, and it is quite easy to curl the wings and shape the
head to make your own version. There is a Japanese legend
that promises a wish to any person who folds 1000 origami
cranes. Why not give it a try?

FLIP 1 45°

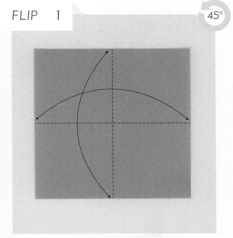

With coloured side up, valley fold and unfold bottom edge to top edge and left edge to right edge. Flip model over and rotate 45 degrees.

2

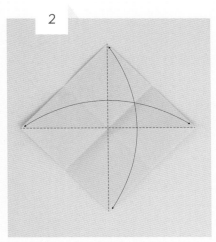

Valley fold and unfold bottom corner to top corner and left corner to right corner.

3

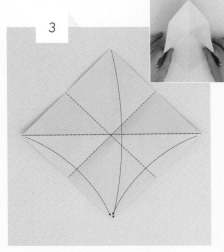

Bring left and right corners down to bottom corner before folding top corner to bottom corner.

4

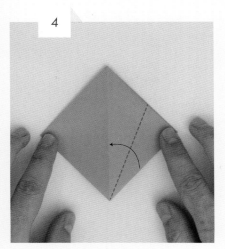

Valley fold right edge of top layer to centre line. Make sure the open flaps of the model are facing down towards you. Repeat on opposite side.

FLIP 5

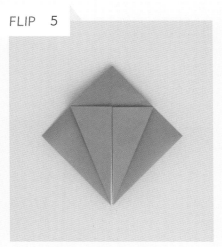

Flip model over and repeat on other side.

6

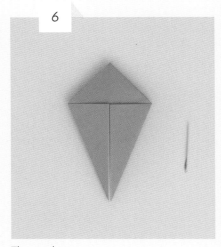

The result.

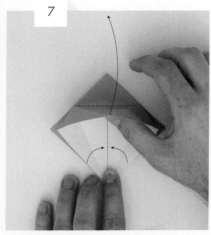

7

Unfold back to diamond shape. With top flap only, fold bottom corner up along line shown while bringing side edges in to meet centre line.

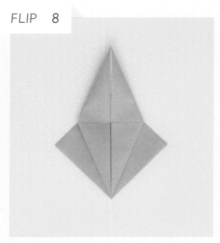

FLIP 8

Flip model over and repeat step 7.

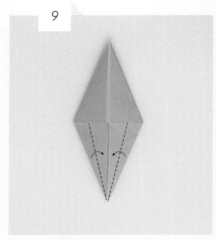

9

Valley fold edges to centre and repeat at the back.

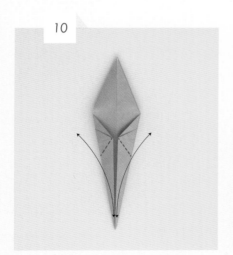

10

Valley fold and unfold each bottom point along lines shown.

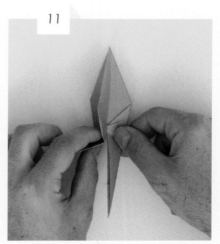

11

Inside reverse fold each point up using previous crease.

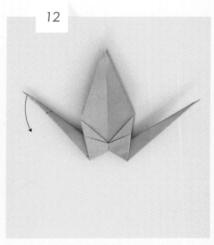

12

Reverse fold head using crease shown and spread wings to create 3D effect.

CROW

The crow is an origami design with many different variations. It's a bird so it would ordinarily start with a bird base, however, I've designed this one by starting with a water bomb base. The challenge with this design is to try and fold it so it stands on its own legs without falling. See if you can get the final folds right to make it stand.

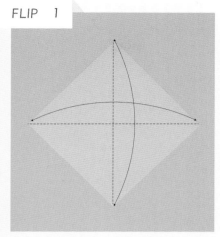

With white side up, valley fold and unfold corners diagonally across centre line on both sides. Flip model.

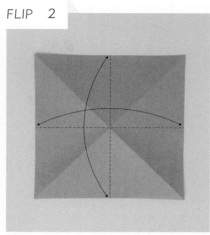

Valley fold and unfold bottom edge to top and repeat from left to right. Flip model.

3

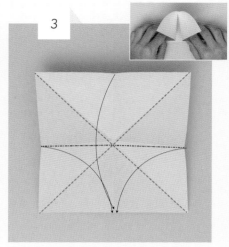

Mountain fold two side edges inwards towards bottom centre point, forming a water bomb base.

4

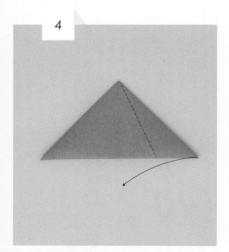

Valley fold top right flap down along line shown. The edge will line up with the centre line.

5

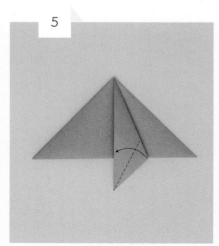

Valley fold right edge in towards centre line.

6

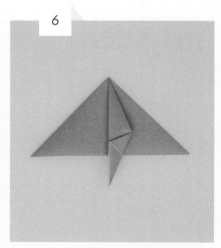

Repeat steps 4 and 5 on top left flap.

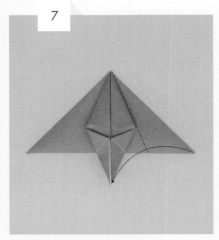

7

Valley fold back right flap down along line shown.

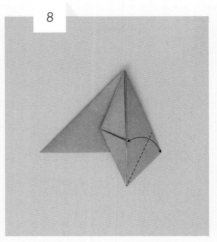

8

Valley fold and unfold bottom right edge inwards towards centre line.

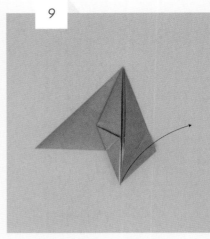

9

Unfold top right flap back to step 7.

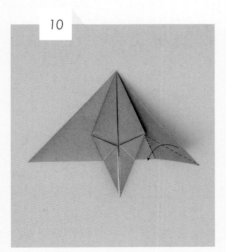

10

Collapse flap along mountain and valley lines shown.

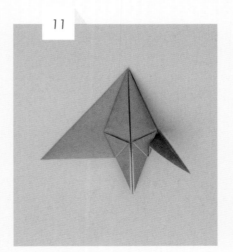

11

Step 10 fold in progress.

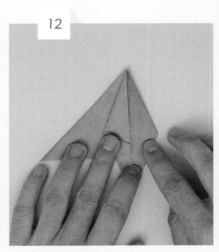

12

Collapse flap all the way down and repeat steps 7–10 on left flap.

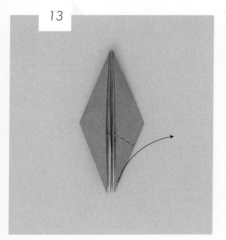

13

Valley fold right flap up along line shown.

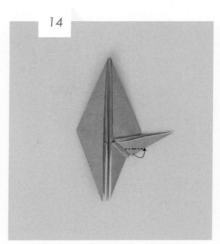

14

Mountain fold bottom of flap along line shown.

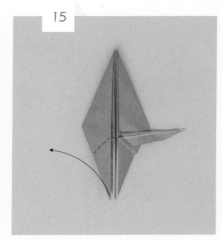

15

Repeat steps 13 and 14 on left flap.

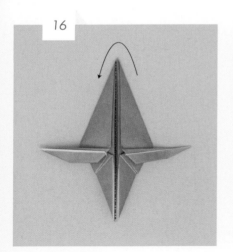

16

Fold model in half.

17

Lay model flat and rotate 90 degrees anti-clockwise.

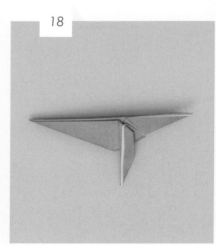

18

The result.

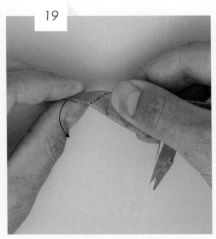

Hold the tip of the model and fold it down along the valley and mountain lines shown to form head.

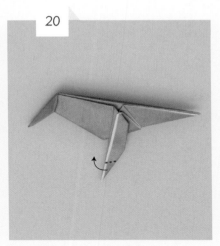

Inside reverse fold bottom flap up along line shown to form foot.

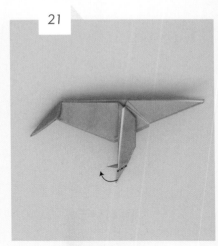

Repeat on opposite foot.

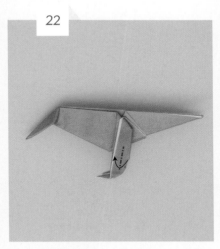

Make leg thinner by making a mountain fold along the outside of leg.

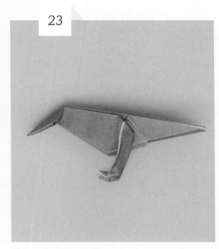

The completed crow.

BUTTERFLY

To me, one of the most elegant yet simple folds is the
traditional butterfly. You begin with the water bomb base
– a starting base for many great designs – and end up with
an origami shape that can be placed around the house as a
decoration or hung from a baby mobile. I find that thin paper,
such as wrapping paper, is best for this design.

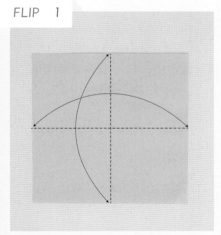

FLIP 1

With coloured side up, valley fold and unfold bottom edge to top edge, folding the paper in half. Fold and unfold left edge to right edge. Flip model over.

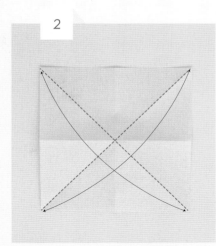

2

Valley fold and unfold bottom left corner to top right corner and bottom right corner to top left corner.

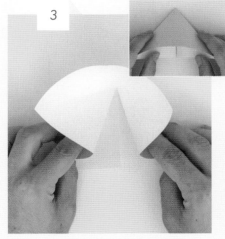

3

Collapse flaps inwards so the model lies flat and forms a triangle.

180° 4

Rotate model 180 degrees.

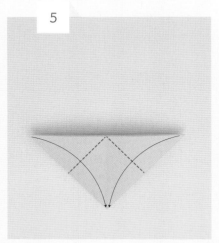

5

Valley fold top layers of top left and right corners to the bottom centre point.

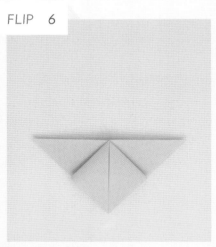

FLIP 6

Flip model over.

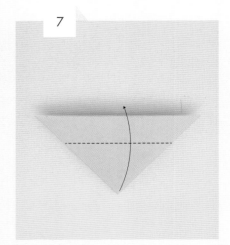

7

Valley fold bottom point up along line shown and fold through all layers.

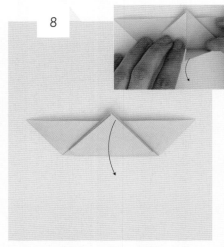

8

Fold down single layer on right-hand side. Place your finger inside the model and press flap down to make model lie flat.

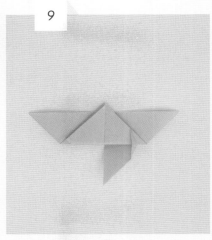

9

Repeat step 8 on the left-hand side.

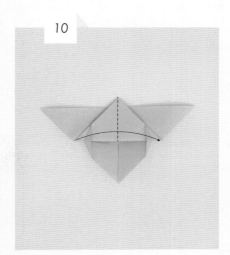

10

Fold model in half.

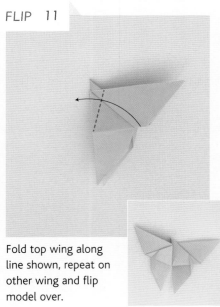

FLIP 11

Fold top wing along line shown, repeat on other wing and flip model over.

12

Fold the tip down to form head. This also acts as a lock to hold the model in place.

POLAR BEAR

The polar bear is one of the first origami animals I designed.
Although simple in shape and quite easy to fold, he definitely
has character. I started with a kite base and created the rest
of the design from there with only a ruler, a bone folder and
some tweezers to help me. Use watercolour paper with a
weight between 160–220gsm.

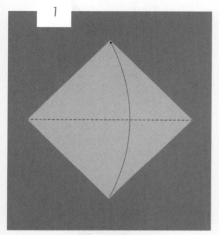

1

With white side up, valley fold bottom corner to top corner.

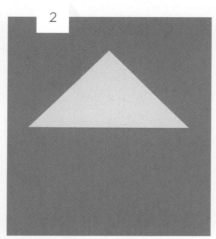

2

Unfold back to previous step.

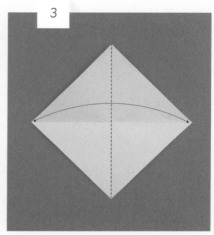

3

Valley fold and unfold left corner to right corner along centre line.

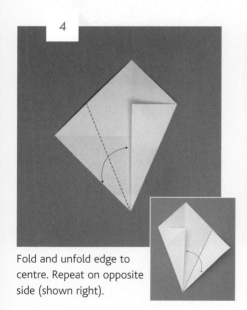

4

Fold and unfold edge to centre. Repeat on opposite side (shown right).

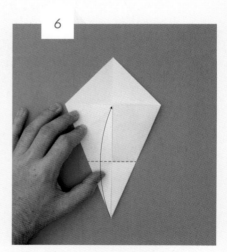

5

Valley fold edges to centre line.

6

Valley fold bottom point to top of raw edges.

7

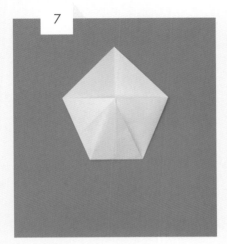

The result.

8

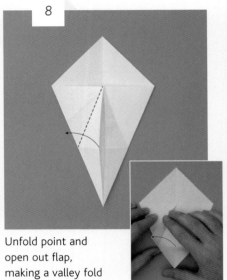

Unfold point and open out flap, making a valley fold along line shown.

9

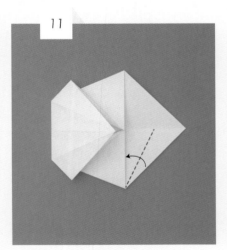

Repeat on opposite side.

90° **10**

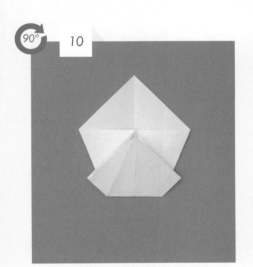

Rotate 90 degrees clockwise.

11

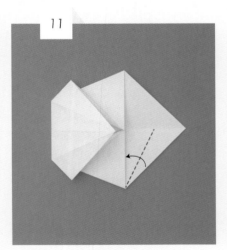

Valley fold raw edge and repeat on opposite side.

FLIP 12 **90°**

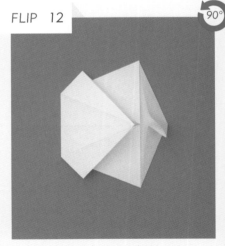

Flip entire model over and rotate 90 degrees anti-clockwise.

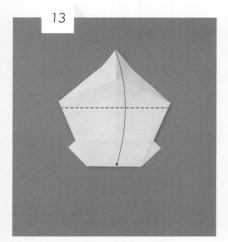

Valley fold top point downwards.

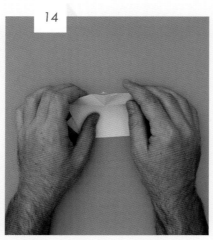

Make sure you catch all the layers and fold firmly.

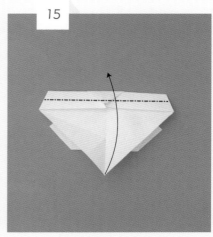

Mountain fold bottom point upward.

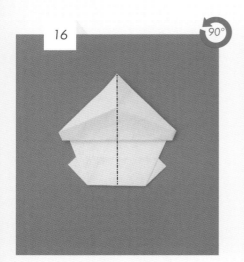

Mountain fold model in half and rotate 90 degrees anti-clockwise.

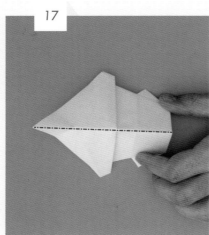

The result.

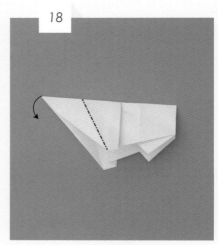

Bring point down, folding a mountain fold along line shown.

19

Repeat on opposite side.

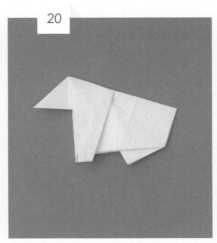

20

The result.

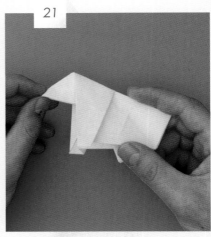

21

Shape nose by folding tip underneath and back towards model.

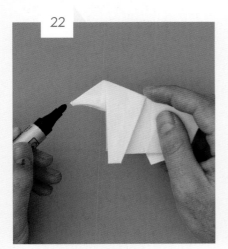

22

Use a black pen to colour nose.

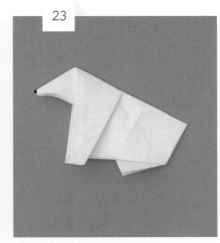

23

The completed polar bear.

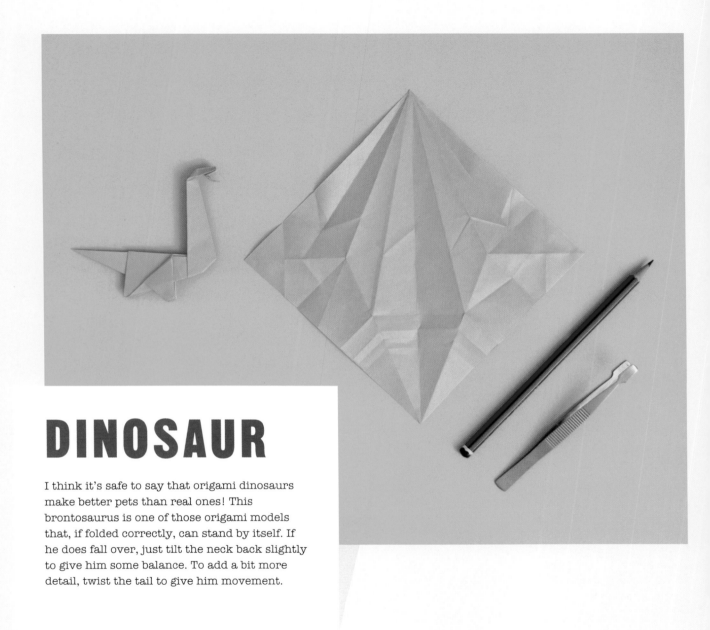

DINOSAUR

I think it's safe to say that origami dinosaurs make better pets than real ones! This brontosaurus is one of those origami models that, if folded correctly, can stand by itself. If he does fall over, just tilt the neck back slightly to give him some balance. To add a bit more detail, twist the tail to give him movement.

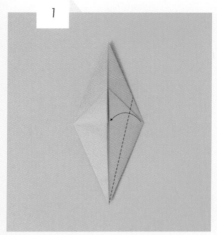

1

Start with a fish base (see page 27), making sure middle flaps are facing up towards top of model. Valley fold right edge to centre line through all layers.

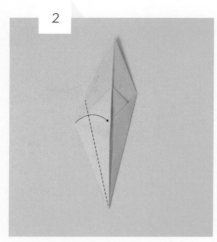

2

Valley fold left edge to centre line.

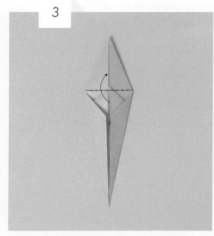

3

Mountain fold back flap along line shown. Use tip of the smaller front flap as reference, but do not fold this flap.

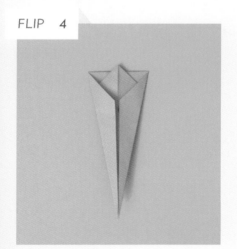

FLIP **4**

Flip model over.

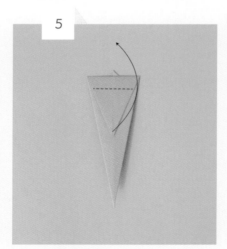

5

Valley fold top flap up along line shown.

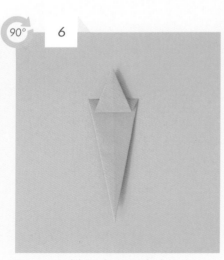

90° **6**

Rotate model 90 degrees clockwise.

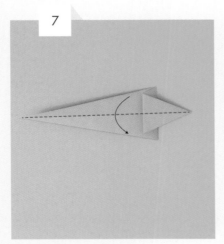

7

Valley fold model in half.

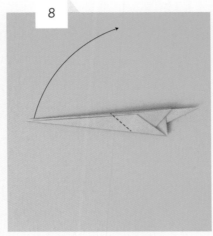

8

Outside reverse fold flap along line shown.

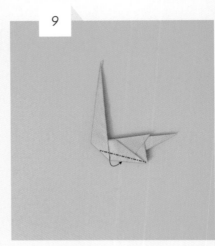

9

Mountain fold bottom flap inside model along line shown.

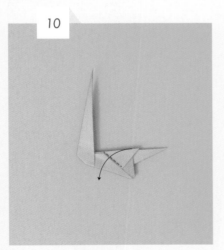

10

Valley fold top flap along line shown and repeat behind.

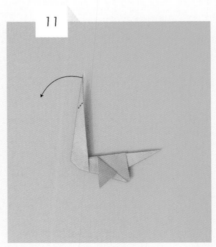

11

Outside reverse fold tip down.

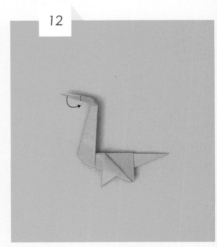

12

Valley fold tip all the way in to form head.

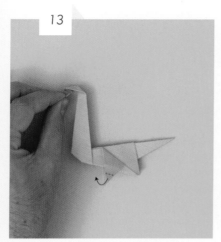

13

Pull out small flap inside head to form mouth. Tuck in bottom corner to form feet on both front legs.

14

The completed dinosaur.

HORSE

Why the long face? I did not use any traditional bases for this design. Instead I tried to portray the essence of the horse in the shape of the face and pointy white ears. Reversing the paper so the white shows through is important to bring out the ear and nose details. You can add eyes and even nostrils to give it more character, if you like.

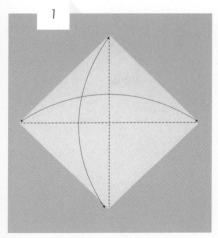

1

With white side facing up and on the diagonal, valley fold and unfold left corner to right corner and bottom corner to top corner through centre.

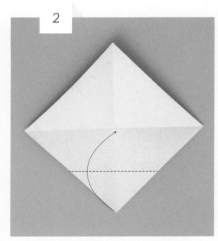

2

Fold bottom corner to centre point.

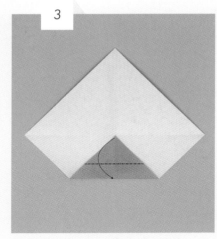

3

Mountain fold point down towards bottom edge.

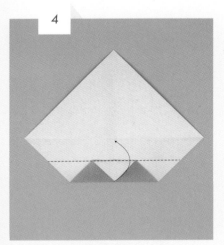

4

Valley fold bottom edge up to centre line along line shown.

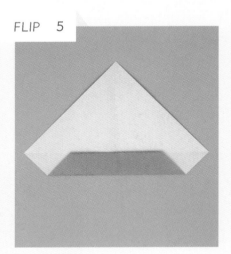

FLIP **5**

Flip model over.

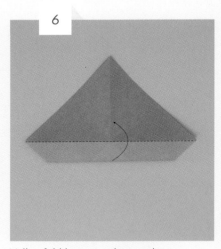

6

Valley fold bottom edge up along centre line.

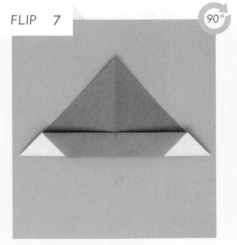

FLIP 7   90°

Flip model over and rotate 90 degrees clockwise.

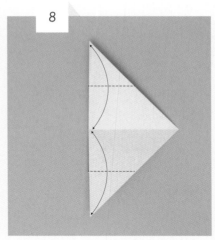

8

Valley fold and unfold top and bottom points to centre line.

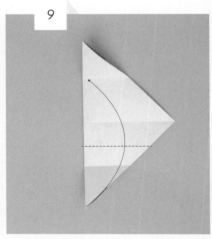

9

Valley fold bottom point up to line made in previous step.

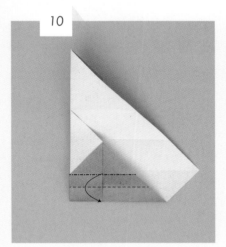

10

Mountain and valley fold top layer along lines shown.

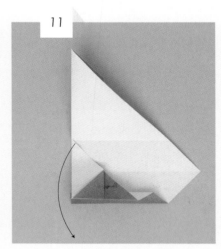

11

Unfold top layer down along mountain fold made in previous step.

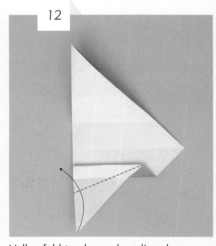

12

Valley fold top layer along line shown.

13

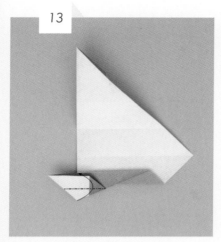

Mountain fold bottom point up along
line shown.

14

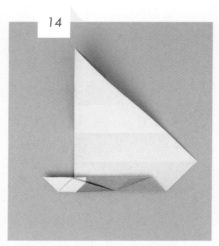

Repeat steps 9–13 on opposite flap.

90° 15

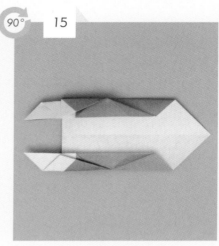

Rotate model 90 degrees clockwise.

16

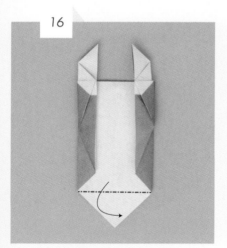

Mountain fold along line shown.

17

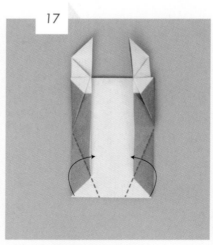

Valley fold side edges in along
lines shown.

FLIP **18**

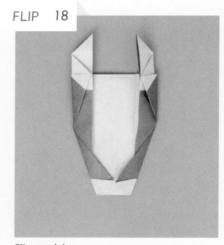

Flip model over.

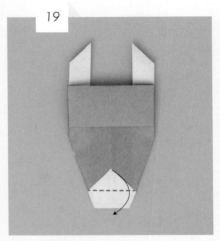

19

Valley fold top layer down below bottom edge. Tuck bottom tip under model.

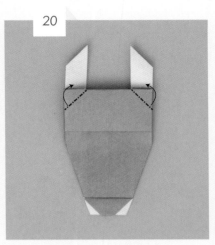

20

Mountain fold top edges below ears.

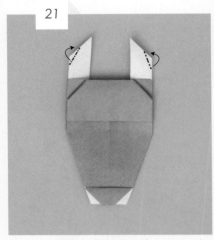

21

Shape ears by tucking the edges around the back.

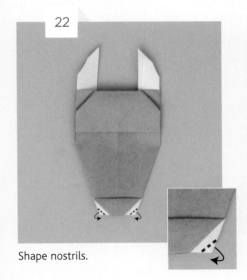

22

Shape nostrils.

23

The completed horse.

ROOSTER

The first time I ever folded an origami chicken I noticed how distinctly square the shape of its head was. When I decided to design a rooster for this book I knew that I wanted to stick with the square head trend that many other roosters have followed because, well, it just looks cool! This design starts with a kite base and if you manage to spread the bottom layers out carefully you can make it stand quite nicely.

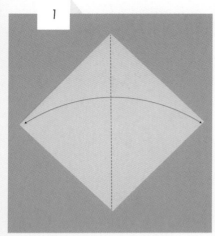

1

With white side facing up and on a diagonal, valley fold and unfold left corner to right corner, folding a line through centre.

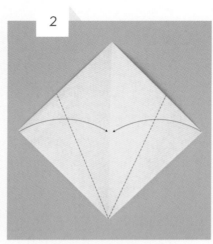

2

Valley fold left and right corners to centre line.

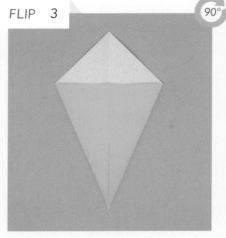

FLIP **3** 90°

Flip model over and rotate 90 degrees clockwise.

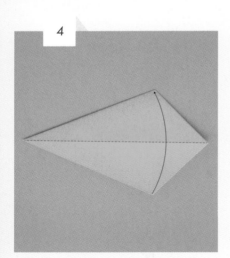

4

Valley fold bottom up along centre line to top.

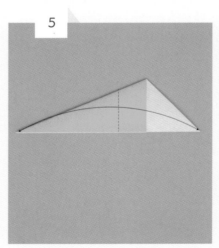

5

Valley fold and unfold left point to right point through centre of model.

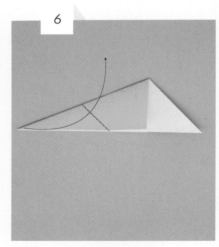

6

Inside reverse fold left point up inside model.

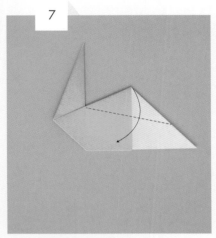

7

Valley fold front flap down along line shown and repeat on opposite side.

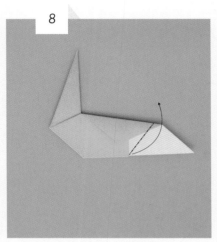

8

Inside reverse fold right flap inside model.

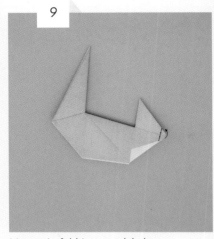

9

Mountain fold into model along line shown.

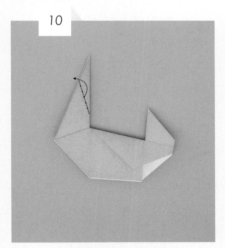

10

Inside reverse fold along line shown to form neck.

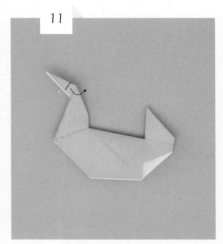

11

Inside reverse fold along line shown to create head.

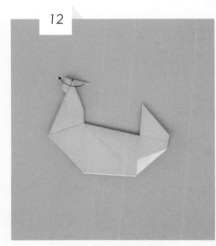

12

Inside reverse fold to create beak and lift wings on both sides.

SEAHORSE

I like this design as it's a sea animal that starts with a fish base. This model is a little challenging when you get to the final steps of creating the curved tail. The tail folds are very subtle, but they bring out the essence of the seahorse, so stick with it!

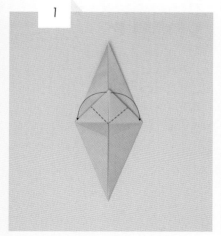

Start with a fish base (see page 27). Valley fold top flaps down along lines shown.

see page 27

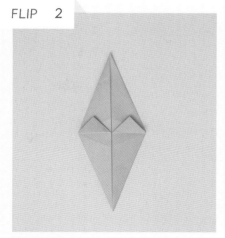

Flip model over.

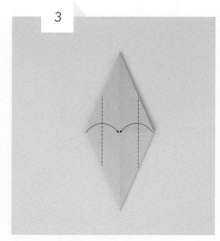

Valley fold left and right points to centre line along lines shown.

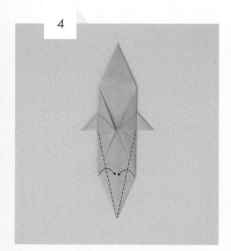

Valley fold right and left edges to centre line along lines shown.

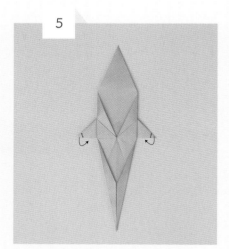

Mountain fold left and right tips into flaps along lines shown.

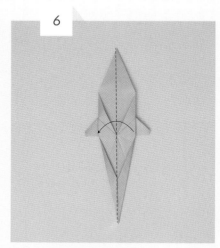

Valley fold model in half.

7

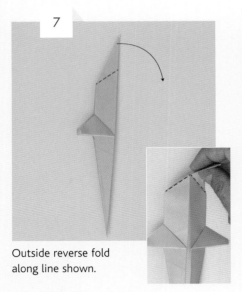

Outside reverse fold along line shown.

8

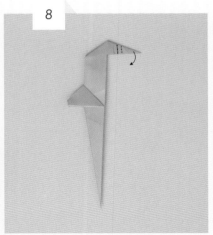

Valley and mountain fold along lines shown to form head.

9

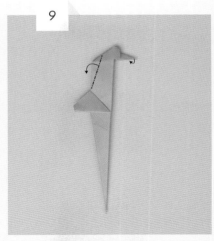

Valley fold tip of the nose into model. Mountain fold back edge into model and repeat on opposite side.

10

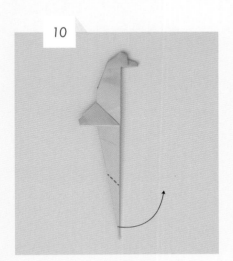

Outside reverse fold bottom tip along line shown.

11

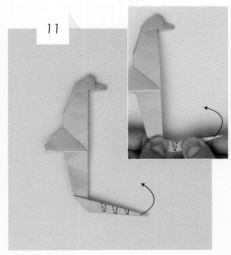

Valley and mountain fold along lines shown to fold little 'notches' into tail. See image inset for example of how to create one notch.

12

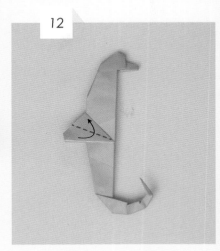

Valley fold fin flap along line shown and repeat on opposite side.

TURTLE

This origami turtle starts with a water bomb base, which is a great base to use when you need a figure with four limbs and a head – the centre point being the head and the four remaining flaps the limbs. Up to the penultimate step, the design is very geometric and rigid. However, by adding a few curls, twists and mountain folds, the flowing shape of the turtle comes to life.

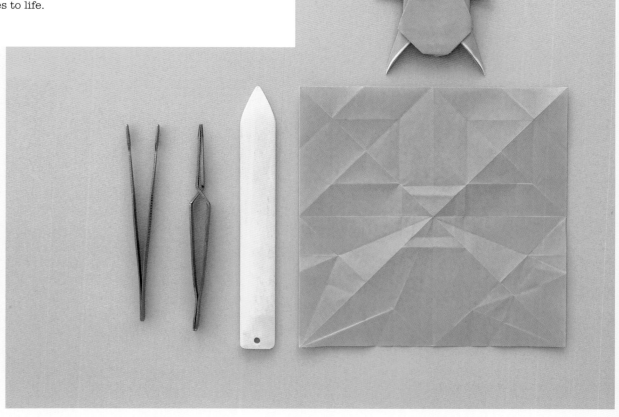

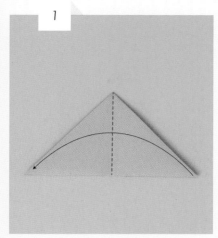

1

Start with a water bomb base (see page 25). Make sure there is a top and bottom flap on both right- and left-hand side. Fold top flap on right-hand side over to the left.

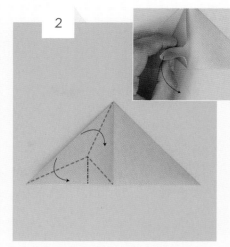

2

Valley fold along lines shown. The edge will meet the centre line and the point of the flap will face up once it lies flat. A mountain fold is formed as you close that flap up.

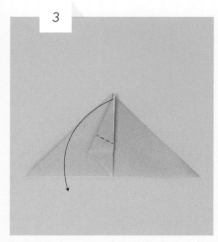

3

Valley fold top point down along line shown.

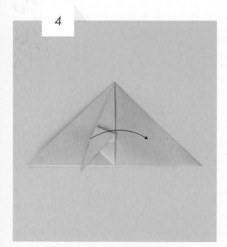

4

Fold completed flap over to the right.

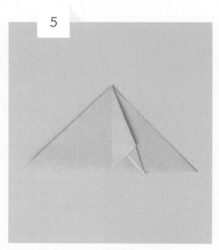

5

Repeat steps 1–4 on left-hand side.

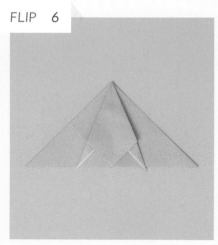

FLIP 6

Flip model over.

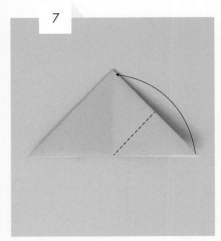

7

Valley fold bottom right point up along line shown.

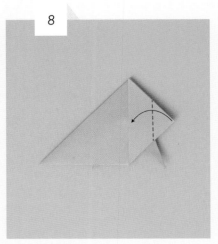

8

Valley fold right point to centre along line shown.

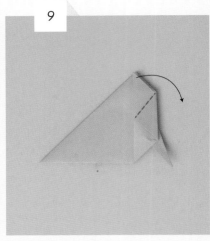

9

Valley fold top point down over previous fold along line shown.

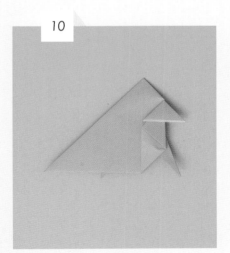

10

Repeat steps 7–9 on left-hand side.

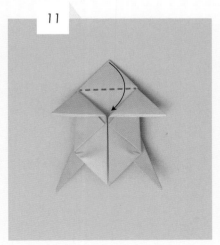

11

Valley fold top point down along line shown.

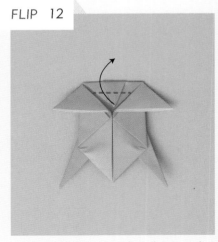

FLIP 12

Valley fold tip up along line shown and flip model over.

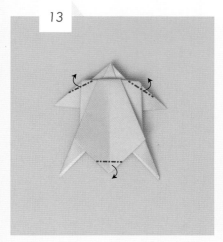

13

To shape the turtle, mountain fold along lines shown, squeeze head and body slightly and curl back legs to create the rounded shape.

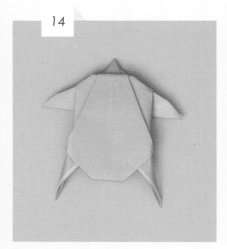

14

The completed turtle.

SWAN

The traditional origami swan is one of the simplest yet most recognisable origami designs. I started with the traditional swan base and added some more details to make this one unique. Creating the feather/wing effect was something I focused on and managed to achieve by folding multiple layers together at the beginning of the folding sequence. This model will work best with thinner paper.

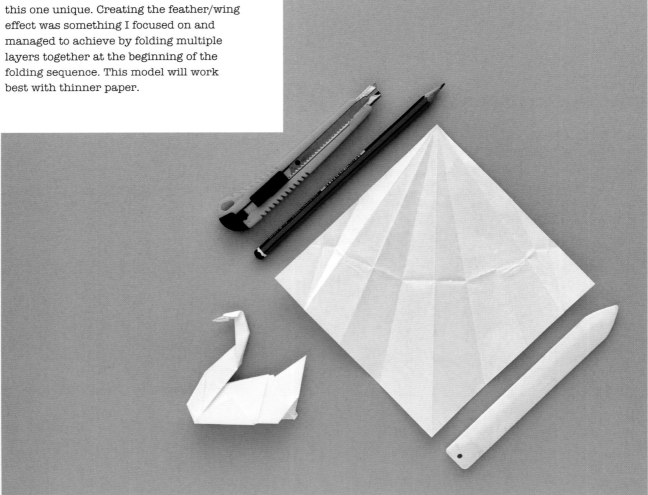

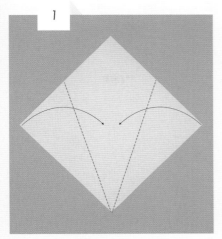

1

Valley fold both points to centre to form a kite base.

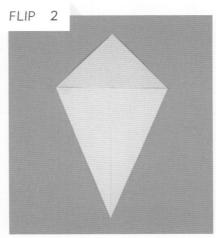

FLIP **2**

Flip model over.

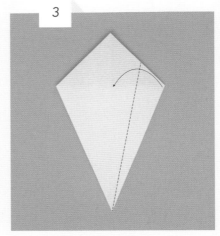

3

Valley fold right flap to centre.

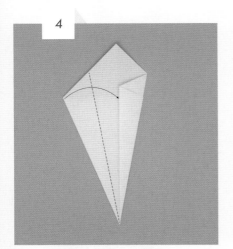

4

Valley fold left flap to centre.

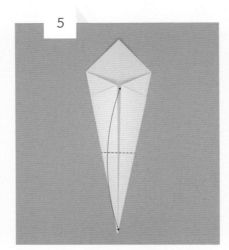

5

Valley fold and unfold bottom point up to where the two upper flaps meet.

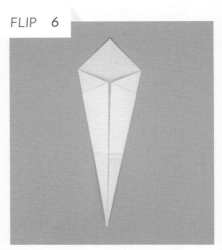

FLIP **6**

Flip model over.

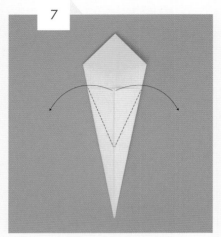

7

Fold top flaps out along line shown. The bottom of the crease will end at the crease made in step 5.

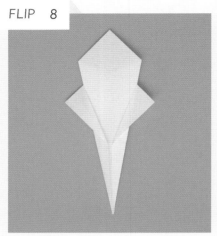

FLIP 8

Flip model over.

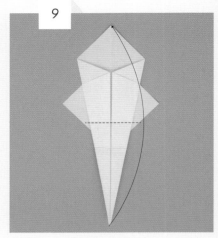

9

Velley fold bottom point up to top point.

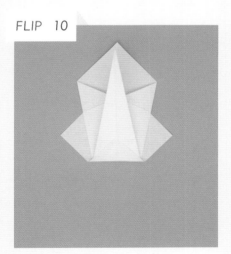

FLIP 10

Flip model over.

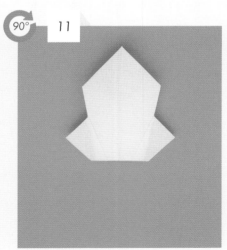

90° 11

Rotate 90 degrees clockwise.

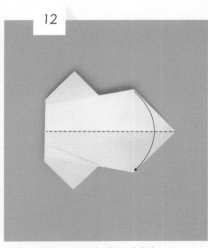

12

Valley fold top half of model down through centre.

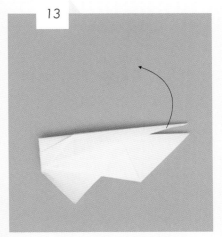

13

Pull top flap up slightly, away from bottom flap.

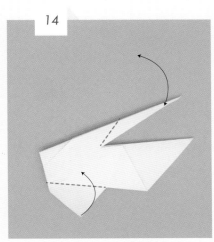

14

Valley fold bottom flap up for the wing and repeat on opposite side. Valley fold and unfold top flap along line shown.

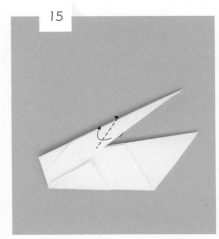

15

Outside reverse fold neck along crease created in previous step.

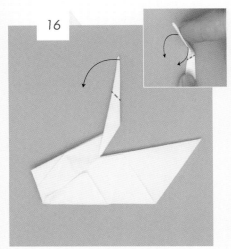

16

Fold top flap down along line shown. Outside reverse fold head shape.

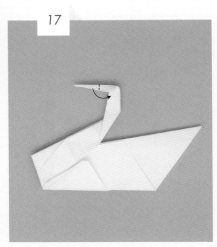

17

Valley fold tip along line shown to form head.

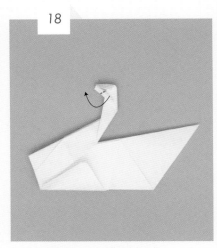

18

Fold tip back out to form beak.

19

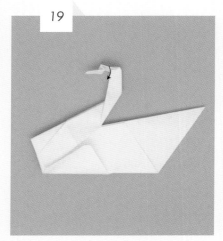

Close up top part to form completed swan head.

20

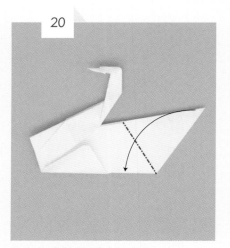

Reverse fold tip of the tail down into model.

21

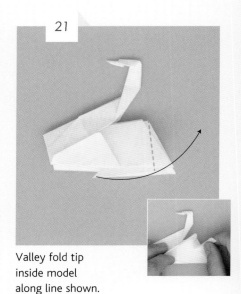

Valley fold tip inside model along line shown.

22

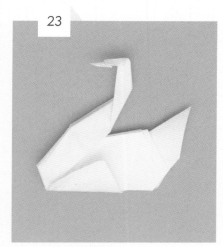

Mountain fold front back flap and repeat on opposite side. Fold front section into model to shape breast.

23

The completed swan.

MANTA RAY

My friend Sipho Mabona (a fellow origami artist) suggested I try to design a manta ray for this book and I'm really glad I did. A manta ray is one of the most fascinating beasts of the ocean. The word 'manta' comes from the Spanish for cloak or shawl, which is what the manta ray looks like as it glides through the water. What's great about this design is how the wings and tail allow you to give it a sense of motion.

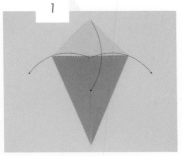

1

Start with a kite base. Open up closed flaps and valley fold top point down along line shown.

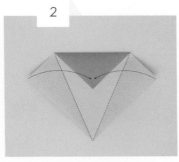

2

Close up model by folding two edge points towards centre line.

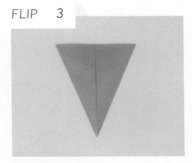

FLIP **3**

Flip model over.

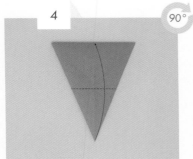

4 90°

Valley fold bottom point up to top edge and rotate 90 degrees clockwise.

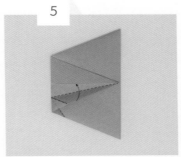

5

Valley and mountain fold bottom flap up to meet centre line.

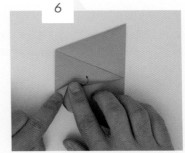

6

Use your index finger to guide fold down onto valley fold and flatten model.

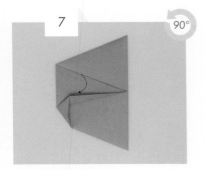

7 90°

Repeat on opposite flap and rotate 90 degrees anti-clockwise.

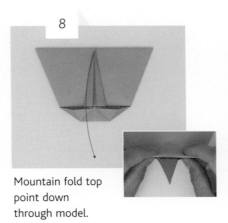

8

Mountain fold top point down through model.

9

FLIP **9**

Flip model over.

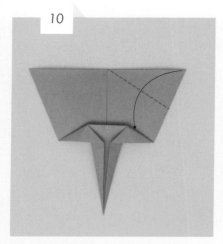

10

Valley fold top right corner down along line shown and repeat on opposite side.

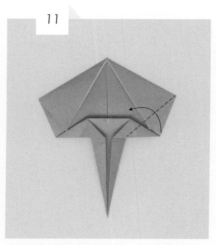

11

Valley fold bottom right corner along line shown. Repeat on opposite side.

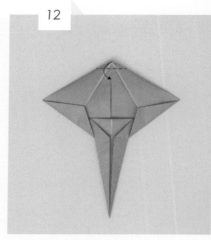

12

Valley fold tip down along line shown.

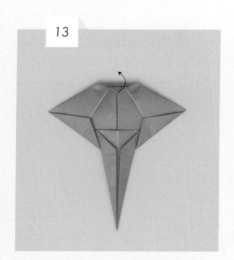

13

Mountain fold tip up along line shown.

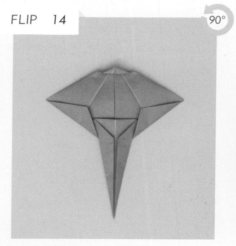

FLIP **14** 90°

Flip model over and rotate 90 degrees anti-clockwise.

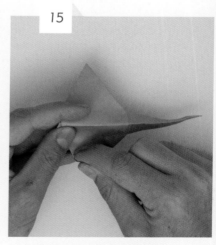

15

Lift model up and squeeze tail to give it shape. Shape fins by curling them up.

OWL

Origami designs can either be flat and two dimensional or three dimensional. This affects what they will look like when photographed. I've tried to take photos of folded origami figures and what I fold and what appears in my photographs are often two completely different things. This origami owl is great because it is simple to fold and simple to photograph. You could also frame one of these to give as a cute gift for a friend.

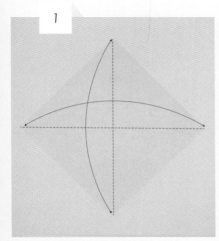

1

With white side facing up and on a diagonal, valley fold and unfold left point to right point and bottom point to top point along centre line.

2

Valley fold top point to centre line, make a pinch mark and unfold. Do not fold along the entire line.

3

Valley fold top point to pinch mark made in previous step.

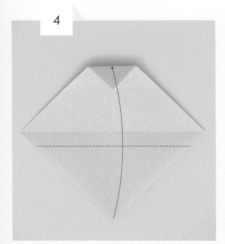

4

Valley fold bottom point up to top edge through line shown.

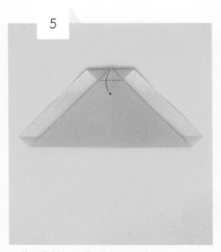

5

Valley fold top flap's point down so it's in line with flap behind.

FLIP **6**

Flip model over.

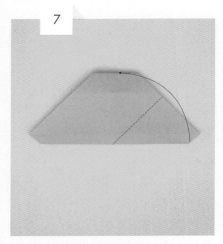

7

Valley fold bottom right corner up to top edge along centre.

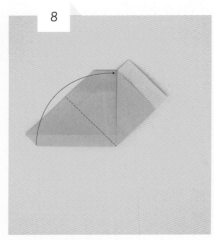

8

Repeat on left-hand side.

FLIP 9

Flip model over.

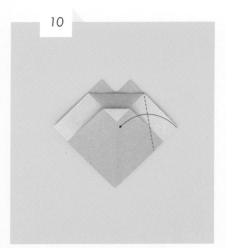

10

Valley fold right corner in along line shown.

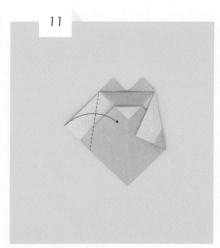

11

Repeat on left-hand side.

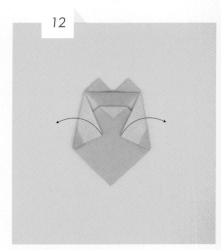

12

Unfold both corners.

FLIP 13

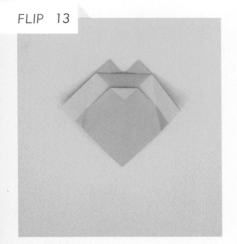

Flip model over.

14

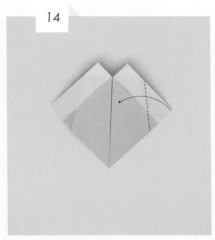

Valley fold right flap along previous crease line.

15

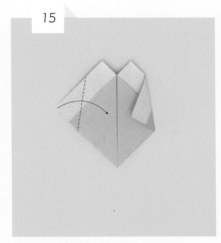

Repeat on left-hand side.

16

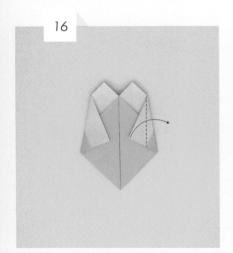

Valley fold right flap along line shown.

17

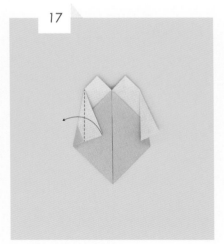

Repeat with left flap.

FLIP 18

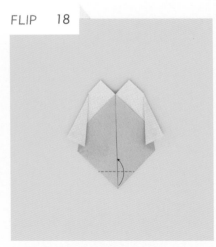

Valley fold bottom point up along line shown and flip model over.

19

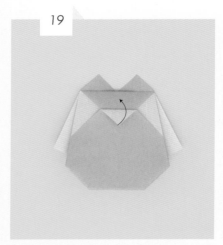

Fold point up along creased line made in step 5.

20

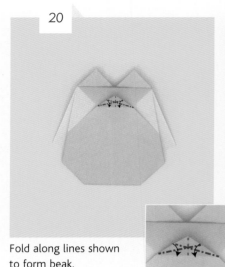

Fold along lines shown to form beak.

21

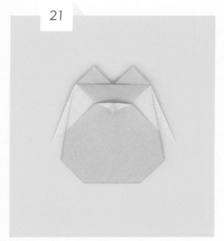

Use a pen to draw big eyes onto the owl.

22

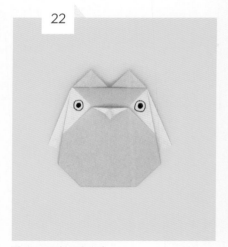

The completed owl.

FOX

I originally wanted to fold a full-figured fox, but when I started with the design it came out quite a lot like the rabbit in this book, so I decided to go with just the head. These kind of models are great for framing or even to use as a mask. Maybe next time you have a Halloween party, fold yourself a fox mask!

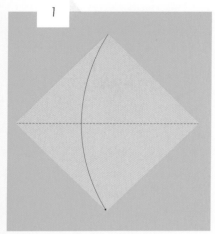

1

With white side facing up and on a diagonal, valley fold top point down to bottom point.

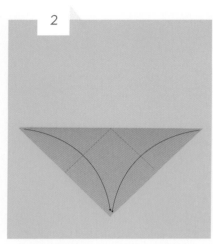

2

Valley fold right corner down to bottom point and repeat on opposite side.

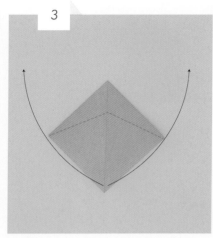

3

Valley fold top flap up along line shown and repeat on opposite side.

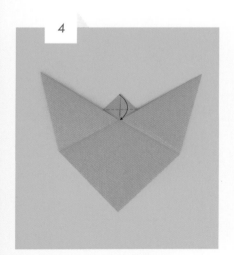

4

Valley fold top point down along line shown.

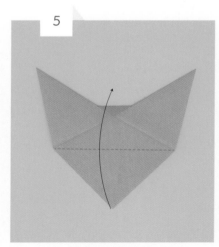

5

Valley fold bottom flaps up along line shown.

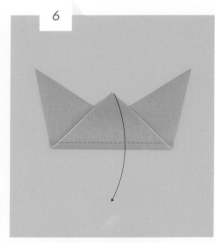

6

Valley fold both flaps down along line shown.

7

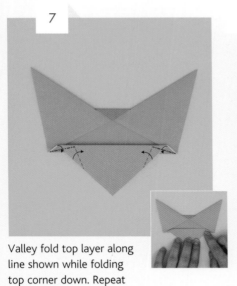

Valley fold top layer along line shown while folding top corner down. Repeat on both sides.

FLIP 8

Flip model over.

9

Valley fold tip of nose up along line shown.

10

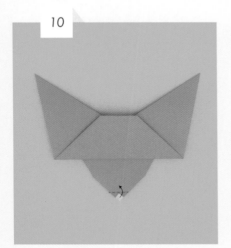

Valley fold tip up along line shown.

11

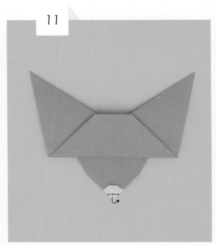

Mountain fold bottom point to form final shape of nose.

12

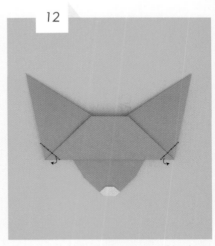

Mountain fold bottom corners of both ears.

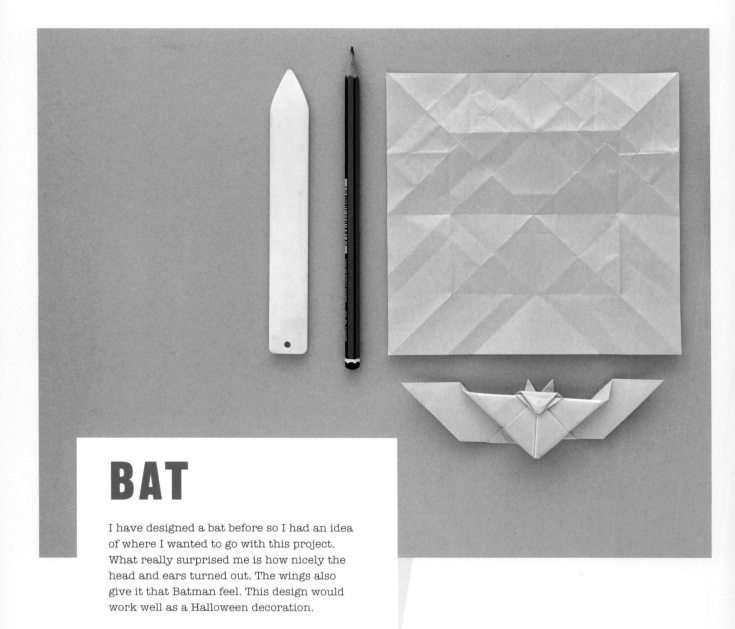

BAT

I have designed a bat before so I had an idea of where I wanted to go with this project. What really surprised me is how nicely the head and ears turned out. The wings also give it that Batman feel. This design would work well as a Halloween decoration.

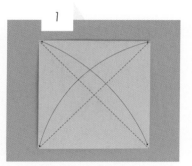

1

Make a water bomb base (see page 25).

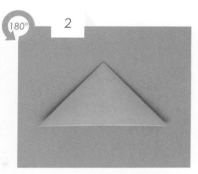

2 180°

Rotate model 180 degrees.

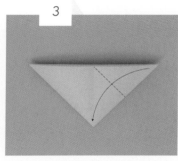

3

Valley fold top right flap down to bottom point and repeat on left-hand side.

FLIP **4**

Flip model over.

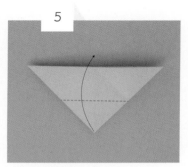

5

Valley fold through all layers along line shown.

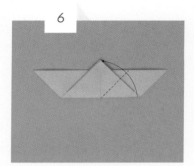

6

Valley fold bottom right edge up to centre point along line shown.

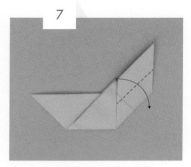

7

Valley fold flap down along line shown.

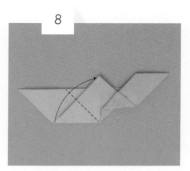

8

Repeat steps 6 and 7 on left-hand side.

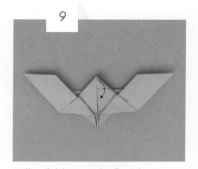

9

Valley fold top right flap down along line shown.

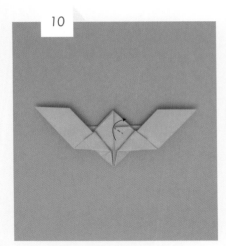

10

Valley fold small flap along line shown.

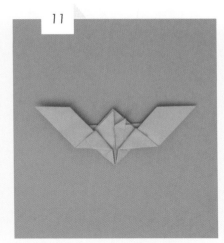

11

Repeat steps 9 and 10 on top left flap.

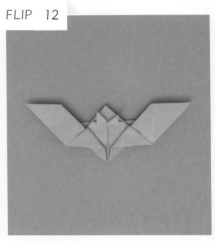

FLIP 12

Flip model over.

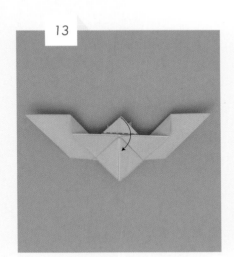

13

Valley fold top down along line shown to make head.

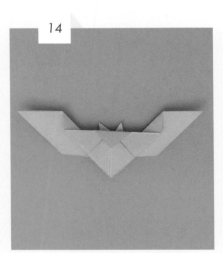

14

Create eye detail by placing your fingers inbetween two flaps on top triangle and opening them up slightly.

15

Press top of the head down slightly to further form eyes.

FISH

You would think that because this design is a fish that you would start with a fish base, right? Wrong! The beauty of origami is that you can use any standard base to create many shapes and figures. For this fish I started with the book base or cupboard base and finished with the windmill base.

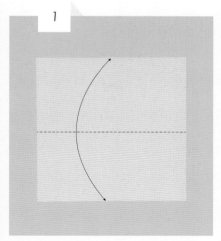

1

With white side facing up, valley fold and unfold top edge to bottom edge through centre.

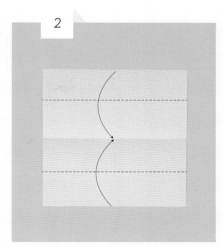

2

Valley fold both edges in towards centre line.

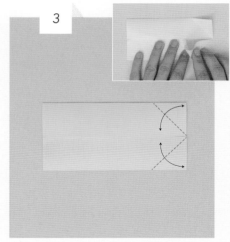

3

Valley fold and unfold the corners along lines shown and inside reverse fold both corners.

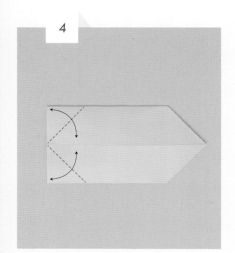

4

Repeat previous step on opposite side.

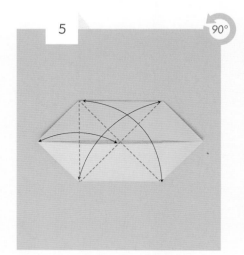

5 90°

Valley fold and unfold along lines shown and rotate model 90 degrees anti-clockwise.

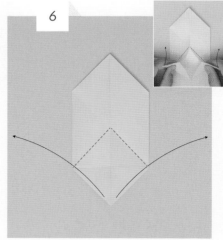

6

Valley fold top two flaps at bottom of model along lines made in step 5.

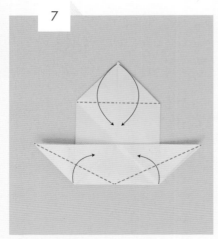

7

Valley fold bottom two flaps up and fold top layer of top two flaps down along lines shown.

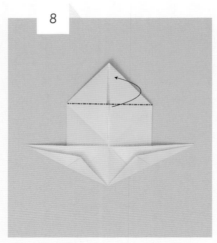

8

Mountain fold top flap behind model.

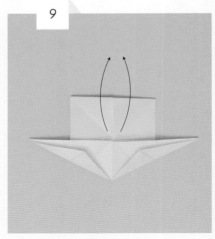

9

Valley fold top two flaps you folded down in step 7 back to their original position.

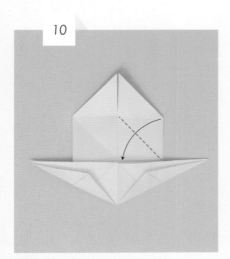

10

Fold top right flap down along line shown.

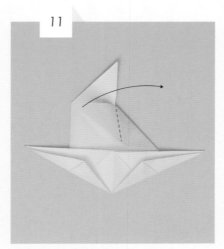

11

Fold top flap along line shown.

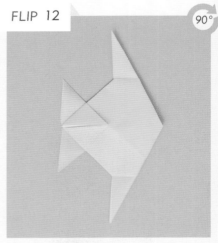

FLIP 12

90°

Repeat steps 10 and 11 on opposite flap, flip model over and rotate 90 degrees clockwise. You can also add a little eye to give the fish character.

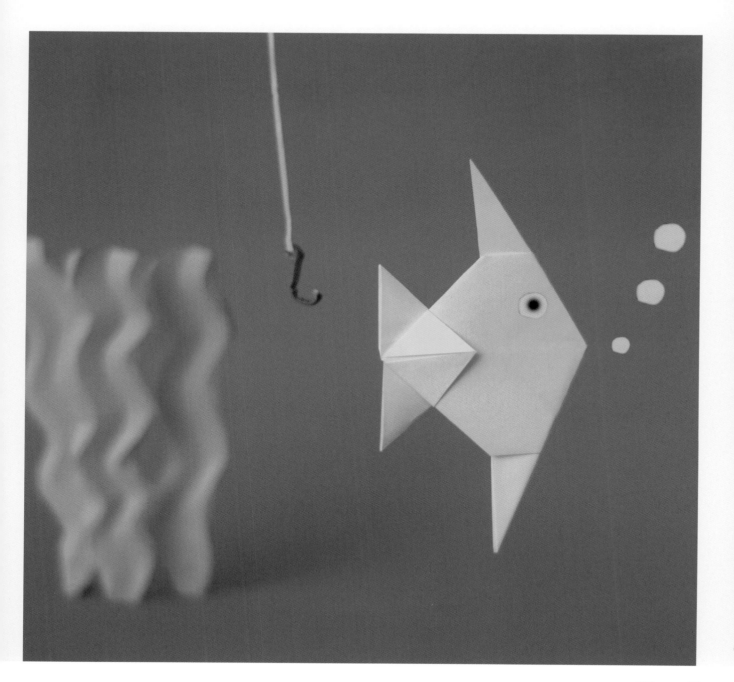

RHINO

There are sadly not too many of these amazing animals left on the planet, but now that you have these instructions you can fold as many of them as you wish! If you want to, you could draw some eyes or change the colour of the horn to make your rhino more unique. You can also adjust the horn's length by folding the final crease up along the tip.

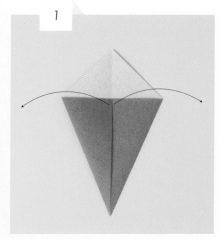

1

Start with a kite base, then unfold model back out to a square.

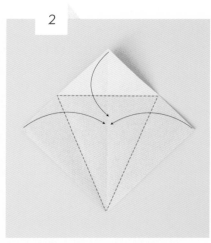

2

Valley fold top point down along line shown (this should be inside the model once all flaps are folded). Valley fold left and right flaps in along creases made in step 1.

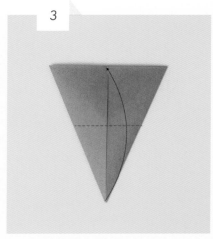

3

Valley fold bottom point up to top edge.

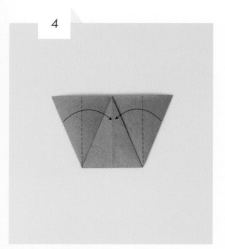

4

Valley fold left and right edges in to meet centre point along lines shown.

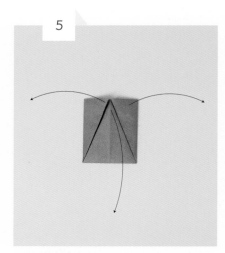

5

Open up all flaps.

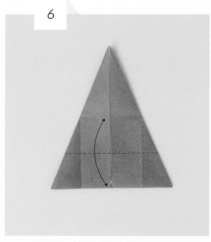

6

Valley fold and unfold bottom edge up to centre line.

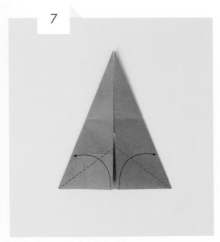

7

Valley fold left and right flaps out to meet edges.

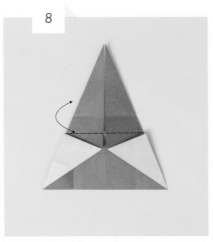

8

Mountain fold and unfold entire model along line shown to form a crease.

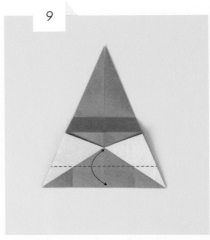

9

Valley fold and unfold along line shown.

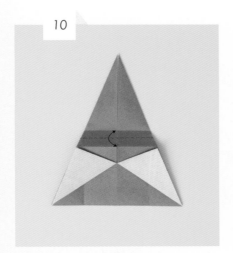

10

Valley fold and unfold through line shown.

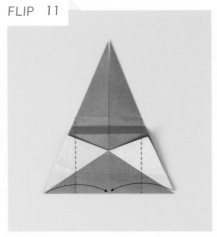

FLIP **11**

Valley fold left and right corners to centre line and flip model over.

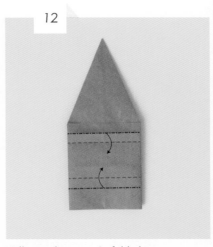

12

Valley and mountain fold along lines shown.

Flip model over and rotate it 90 degrees clockwise.

14

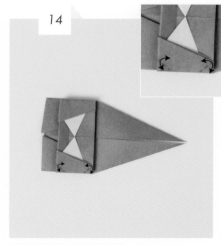

Valley fold and unfold bottom corners along lines shown.

15

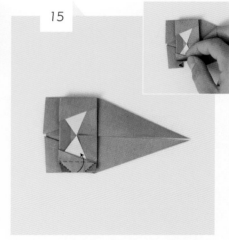

Mountain fold bottom edge up along lines shown. The valley fold from the previous step becomes a hinge to fold bottom edge up over.

16

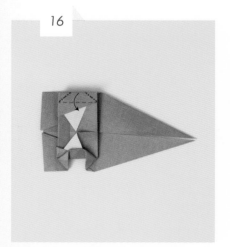

Repeat steps 14 and 15 on top edge.

17

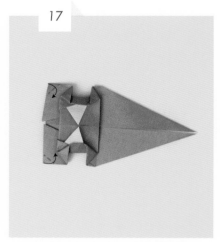

Valley fold corners along lines shown.

18

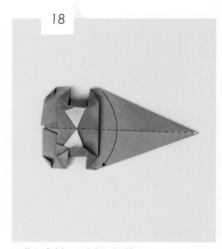

Valley fold model in half.

19

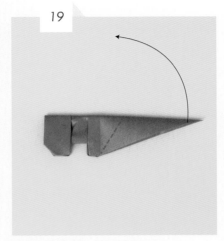

Valley fold tip up along line shown to form crease.

20

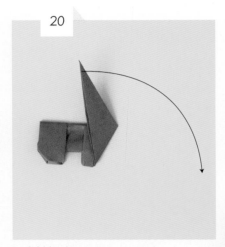

Unfold back to previous step.

21

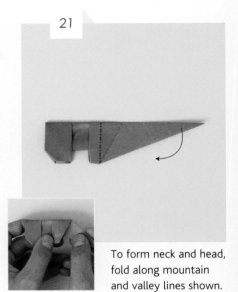

To form neck and head, fold along mountain and valley lines shown. This brings tip down to a lower angle.

22

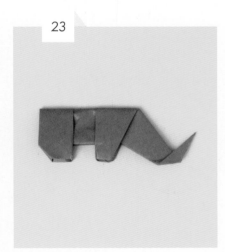

Outside reverse fold tip along line shown to form horn.

23

The completed rhino.

DRAGON

A dragon, what a magnificent beast! Ever since I started designing origami models I wanted to create a dragon. It looks like a crane up until the final few steps, but the details bring out the majestic essence of this mythical creature. You could add more pleats to the wings to give it a little something extra, or even curl them slightly to add movement.

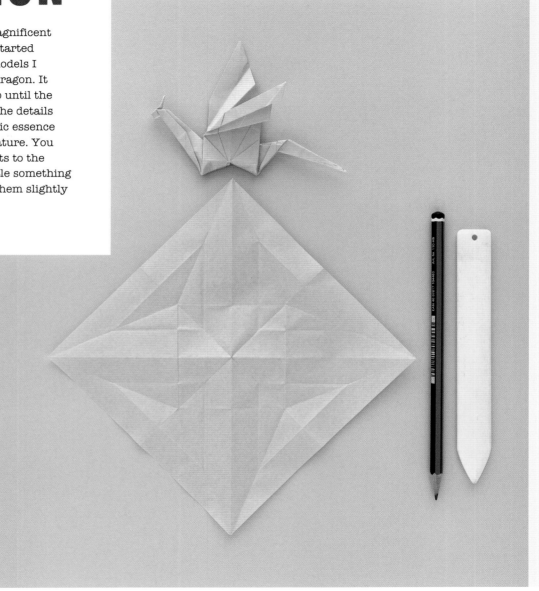

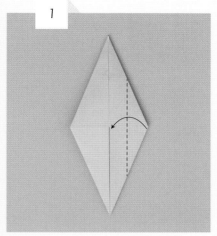

1

Start with a bird base (see page 26).
Valley fold right edge point to centre line.
The fold will be parallel to centre line.

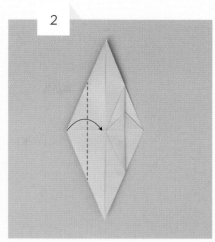

2

Repeat on opposite side.

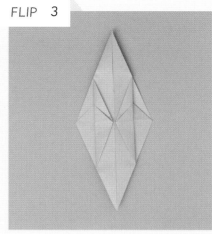

FLIP 3

Flip model over and repeat steps 1 and 2.

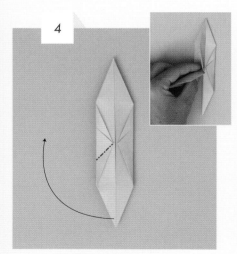

4

Inside reverse fold along line shown.

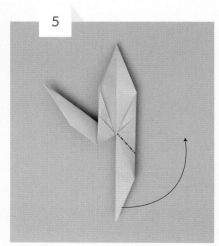

5

Repeat on opposite side.

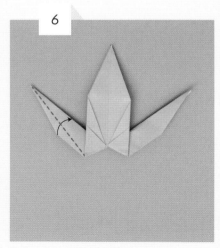

6

Valley fold top left edge up along
line shown.

7

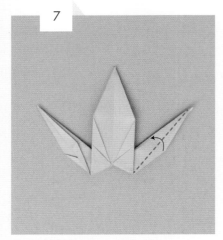

Repeat behind – this will make flaps thinner – and on opposite side.

8

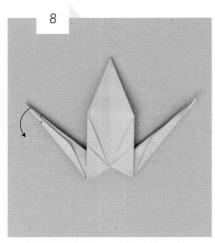

Inside reverse fold tip to form head.

9

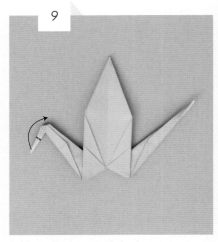

Fold top back towards body to form head.

10

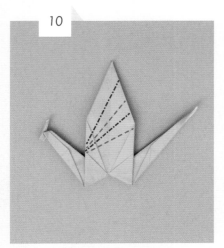

Valley and mountain fold wings down and up along lines shown to form and shape wing.

11

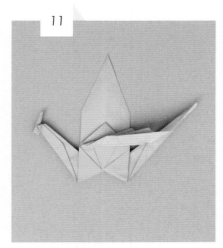

Repeat on opposite wing.

12

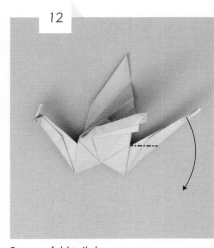

Reverse fold tail down.

13

Pinch and shape front and back legs.

14

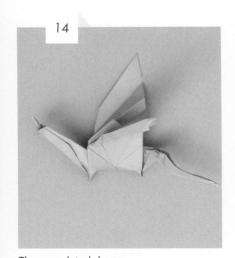

The completed dragon.

RABBIT

This is quite similar to the traditional origami rabbit design in terms of its shape. However, the one I've designed has different ears and more weight in its body. In origami, there are few animals that are easy to capture the essence of, but the rabbit is one of them. This model works best with paper that has the same colour on both sides, but for clarity I have used paper that has a different colour on each side.

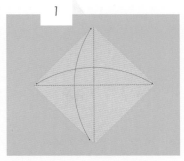

1

On the diagonal, complete steps 1 and 2 of the Crane project (see page 30).

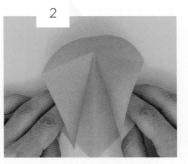

2

Mountain fold two side edges inwards towards bottom centre point.

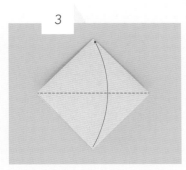

3

Valley fold bottom point of top layer up to top corner.

FLIP 4

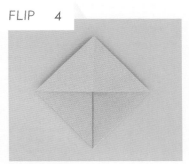

Flip model over.

5 135°

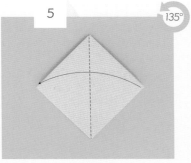

Valley fold in half from right to left and rotate 135 degrees anti-clockwise.

6

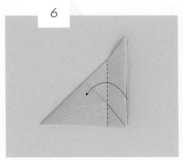

Valley fold top two flaps to the left.

7

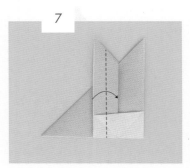

Valley fold top flaps to line shown.

8

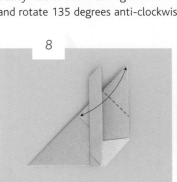

Valley fold and unfold top corner along line shown.

9

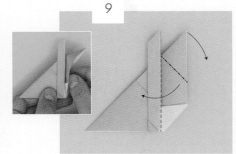

Valley fold front flaps back along line shown while bringing point down along mountain fold indicated.

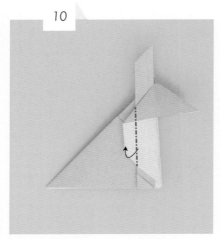

10

Mountain fold top flap into the model.

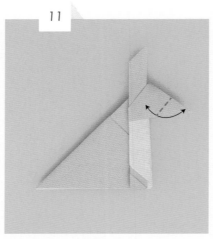

11

Valley fold and unfold top corner along line shown.

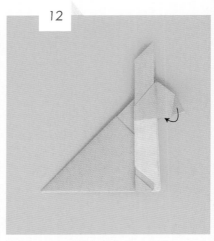

12

Inside reverse fold tip into model to form head.

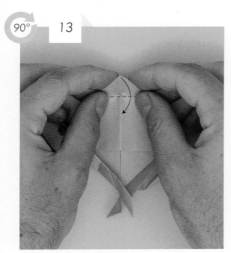

13 90°

Rotate 90 degrees clockwise, open it up like the rabbit is lying on its stomach and valley fold tip down to form tail.

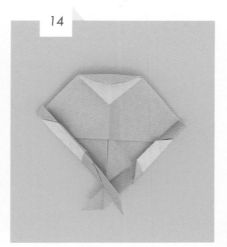

14

Close model up and pull tail out.

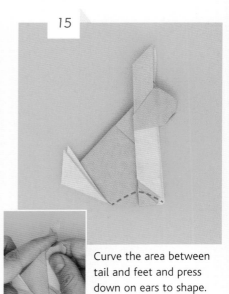

15

Curve the area between tail and feet and press down on ears to shape.

PIG

This was the first design I ever used for an art installation: 250 origami pigs hanging in a restaurant window. The pig can be folded from most paper types, but to give it a bulkier look, try folding it with some watercolour paper (120-200gsm). When I show this design to people they always light up. It has a cheeky personality and, when shaped correctly, it really captures the essence of a pig.

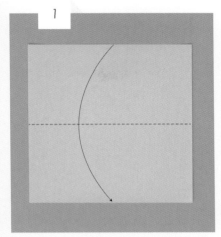

1

With coloured side up, valley fold sheet in half by folding top edge to bottom edge. Align edges as close as possible.

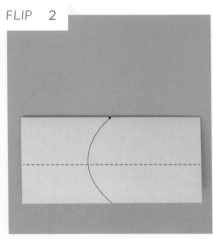

FLIP **2**

Valley fold bottom edge up to centre line, flip model over and repeat on back.

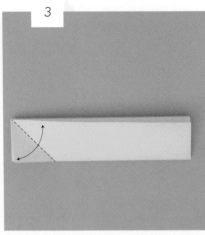

3

Inside reverse fold left corner into model.

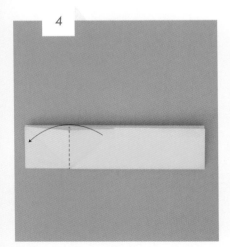

4

The result.

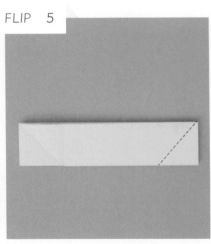

FLIP **5**

Repeat on right corner, then flip model over and repeat on opposite two corners.

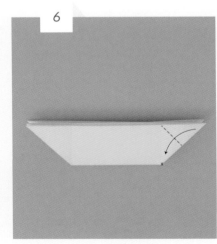

6

Valley fold right corner to crease made in steps 4 and 5. Repeat on back.

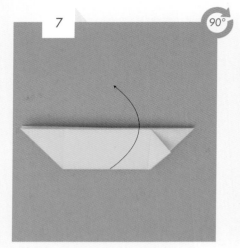

7 ↻90°

Open up model and rotate 90 degrees.

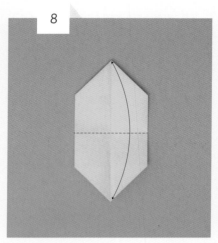

8

Valley fold and unfold top point down to bottom point.

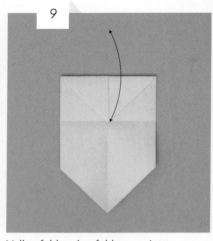

9

Valley fold and unfold top point to crease made in previous step.

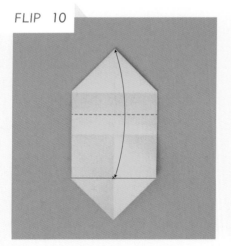

FLIP 10

Valley fold and unfold top point to reference line. Flip model over.

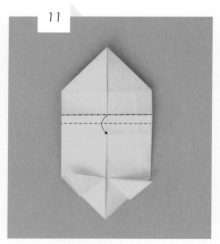

11

Fold mountain fold over valley fold to centre line. This is a pleat fold.

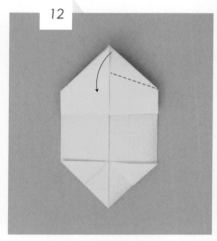

12

Valley fold top right flap down to existing crease line.

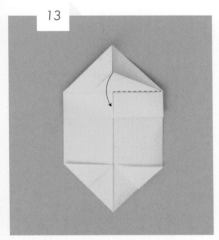

Valley fold entire flap down and fold small triangle inwards.

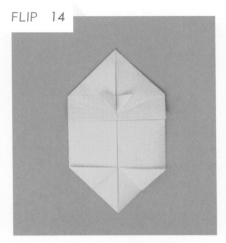

Repeat on left side and flip model over.

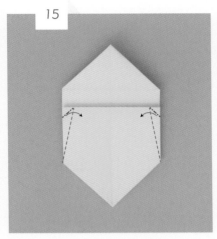

Flip model over. Fold and squash top layers, leaving layer beneath exposed.

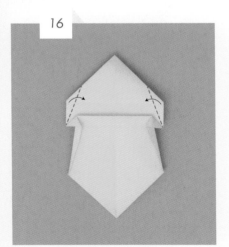

Valley fold corner in and repeat on opposite side.

90°

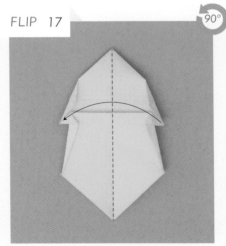

Close model up. Flip model over and rotate 90 degrees.

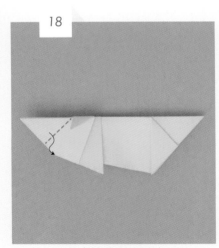

Inside reverse fold along line shown.

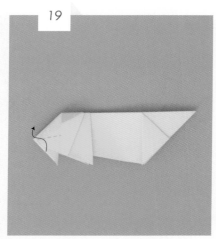

19

Inside reverse fold along inside of model using valley fold shown. Faded valley fold indicates fold inside of model.

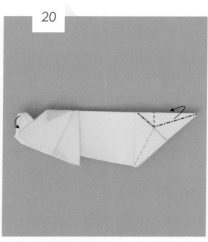

20

Fold the valley and mountain folds using middle tail flap. The faded line indicates fold line inside model, not on outer flap. Fold point of nose down into model to form pig snout shape.

21

Mountain fold back points to form leg. Repeat on both legs. Twist tail, curl ears and pinch trotters.

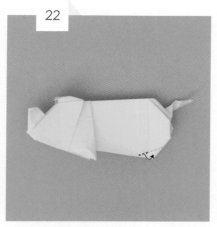

22

Mountain fold bottom layer to form belly and repeat on opposite side.

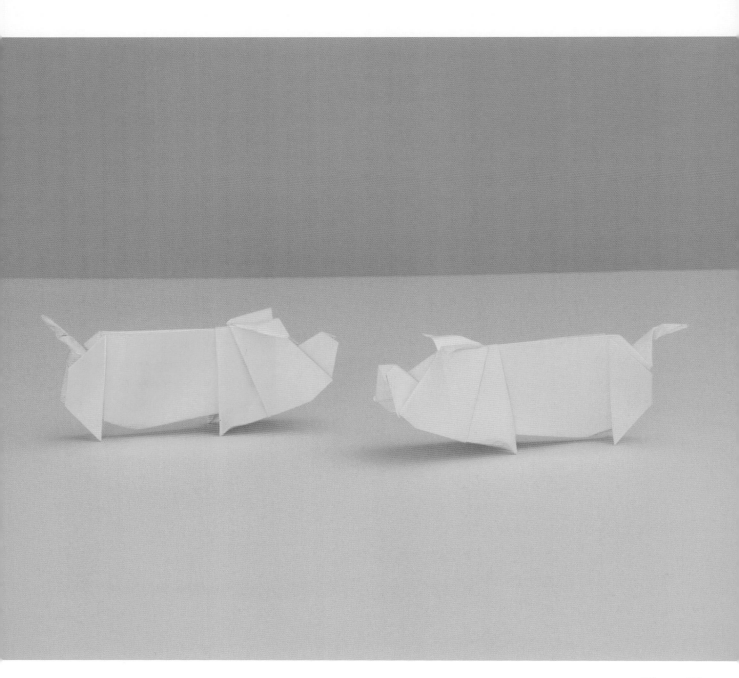

MOUSE

Originally I wanted to design a squirrel using a fish base. I started by creating the long tail and, as I worked on it, I just kept seeing a mouse and so the mouse was born! This design can be folded with thin paper or a heavier weighted paper like watercolour paper.

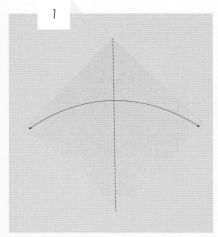

1

With white side up and on a diagonal, valley fold and unfold left and right corners through centre line.

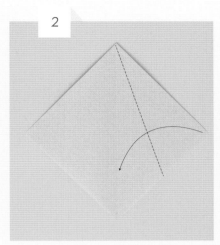

2

Valley fold right flap inwards to lie on centre line and repeat on opposite side.

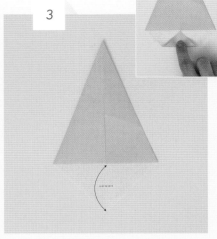

3

Make a pinch mark by valley folding bottom point up to edge of flaps made in previous step and unfold.

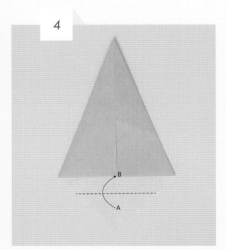

4

Valley fold pinch mark you made in previous step (marked 'A') to point B.

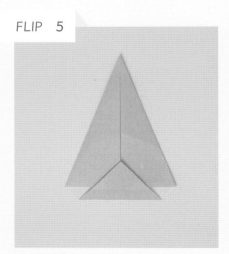

FLIP 5

Flip model over.

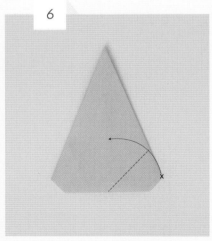

6

Valley fold bottom right corner so that point 'x' lies along centre line of model.

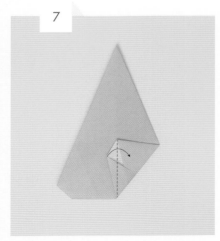

7

Valley fold left side of flap inwards along centre line.

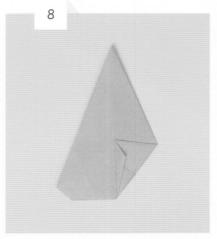

8

Repeat steps 6 and 7 on bottom left-hand corner.

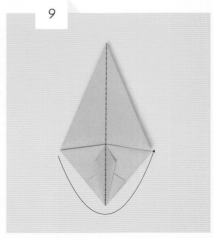

9

Mountain fold model in half.

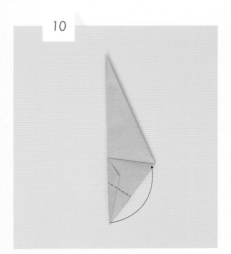

10

Valley fold along line shown.

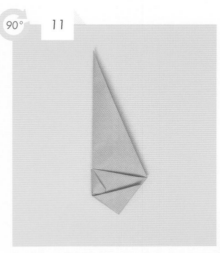

90° **11**

Rotate model 90 degrees clockwise.

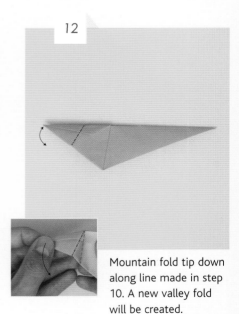

12

Mountain fold tip down along line made in step 10. A new valley fold will be created.

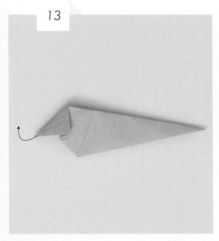

13

Unfold back to previous step and lift up top flap.

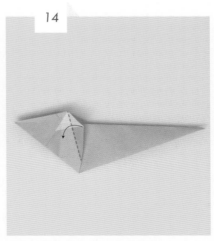

14

Valley fold along line shown.

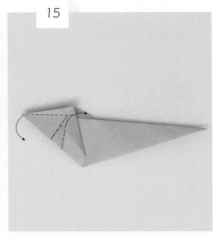

15

Bring tip of nose down using folds made in step 12 while opening ear flap.

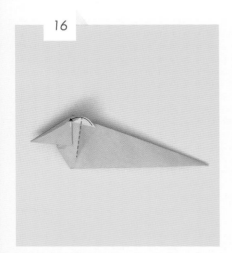

16

Valley fold lightly along line indicated to further form shape of ear. Repeat on opposite ear.

17

Inside reverse fold far right point into model along line shown. The tip of point should stick out below head.

18

The result.

19

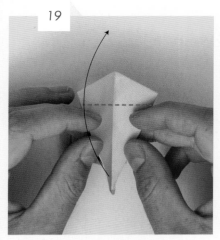

Open up model and valley fold tail up along line shown.

20

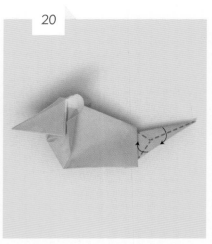

Valley fold along lines shown to make tail thinner.

21

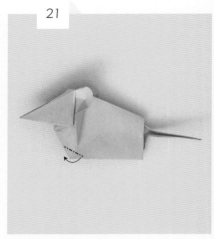

Mountain fold bottom to shape body.

22

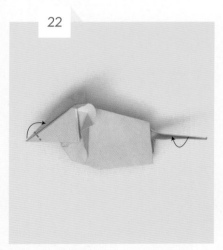

Valley fold front top of model to form nose. Curl to shape tail.

23

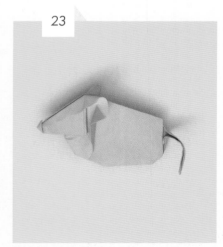

The completed mouse.

INDEX

ACKNOWLEDGMENTS

Turning a hobby into a career is not something that many people get to experience and I feel very grateful that I've been able to do just that. My family and friends have supported me a great deal throughout my transition from day job to origami artist. Thank you to everyone involved in making this book a reality: The Instagram community – without them I would not have been able to make this happen as quickly as it did – and to you, the reader. Thanks for reading *Love Origami!* and supporting me and the origami community.